**To my children Arnaav, Mansi and Ansh,
my papa and my mummy watching from her
heavenly abode.**

About STEM For Kids

Mission: Make STEM fun and real.

STEM For Kids® is the brainchild of Moni Singh. After contributing as an engineer and an industry leader to the development and deployment of various technologies like wireless phones, telecommunications equipment and smart meters, Singh embarked on the mission to expose children to the immense potential, the energy and the excitement in STEM fields.

Her two children, a 1st and a 2nd grader at that time, were Singh's inspirations. One day, making paper bridges with them, she noticed the spark in their eyes as they engineered new and stronger bridge designs. Not only were they deeply engaged, they were hungry for more. Seeing their craving for more hands-on STEM activities, Singh tried to find programs in the area but to no avail. Singh was determined to do something to keep the spark alive for her kids and to create more sparks in young minds in the community. STEM For Kids® was born.

Born and raised with industry, STEM For Kids® is unique in its strong ties to the real world of STEM. Programs are designed by engineers, people in the industry & educators to specifically address "so what" in a hands-on way. An equal emphasis is placed on keeping the programs fun and exciting so children may develop an intrinsic interest in STEM.

The STEM For Kids® curriculum has evolved to over 40 different courses used by thousands of educators serving millions of children worldwide. Like Singh's now 2nd grader (yes! her third child), many generation Alpha kids continue the fun-filled STEM learning experiences.

This STEM Instruction Manual Issued To:

____

IMPORTANT NOTICE:

ISBN: 979-8-9878360-8-8

Table of Contents

Money Smart Kids: Building Financial Foundations

STEM For Kids® Money Smart Kids: Building Financial Foundations introduces students to essential financial literacy skills, helping them navigate earning, saving, budgeting, and smart spending while fostering critical thinking, creativity, collaboration, and financial responsibility.
Through interactive activities, students explore entrepreneurship, decision-making, and long-term financial planning to build a strong foundation for financial success.

Educational Connection

STEM For Kids® 4 Dimensional Learning		
Core Ideas (Standards - what it is)	*Career Connections & Practices (CCP - what to do)*	*Cross-Cutting Concepts (CCC - how it relates)*
Financial Literacy: • Earning Income • Buying Goods and Services • Saving • Using Credit • Financial Investing • Protecting and Insuring Science Standards: • Algorithms and Coding • Motion and Stability: Forces and Interactions • Matter and Its interactions • Engineering Design Information and Communications Technology (ICT): • Computer Systems • Technology as a Tool • Data and Analysis • Networks and the Internet Applied Mathematics: • Make sense of problems and persevere in solving them • Reason abstractly and quantitatively • Look for and make use of structure Applied Language Arts: • Comprehension and collaboration • Presentation of Knowledge and Ideas	Critical Thinking: • Analyze real-world spending decisions to differentiate between needs and wants. • Evaluate the risks and rewards associated with different ways of earning money. • Apply decision trees to assess financial choices. • Assess loan options and repayment strategies for long-term financial commitments. Research: • Investigate various career paths and their financial implications. Collaboration: • Participants are given a job in a group to research and present innovations. • Collaborate in a simulated STEM Market setting to engage customers and manage transactions. Creativity: • Work creatively together with a group of other participants. • Develop creative solutions for budgeting challenges through role-playing exercises. Communication: • Prepare and present information on participant-built projects. • Engage in customer interactions within the STEM Market to practice sales communication. • Share and justify budgeting decisions within group activities. Problem Solving: • Applying the engineering design process to certain goals, criteria, and constraints. • Solve budgeting challenges by prioritizing expenses and managing savings. • Address financial constraints when planning major purchases. Career Connections: • Explore job responsibilities, salaries, and work environments across various careers. • Analyze how financial literacy impacts career choices and long-term financial stability. • Investigate the role of financial planning in different industries.	Systems and Models: • Understand how a budgeting system helps manage personal finances effectively. • Learn the structure of a business model. • Examine the economic systems that influence financial decision-making. • Explore the components of a loan system and how repayment works. Structure and Function: • Identify key elements of financial planning, including income, expenses, savings, and investments. • Understand the role of banks and financial institutions in money management. • Examine the structure of sales tax and its function in economic systems. Patterns: • Recognize spending and saving patterns to develop better financial habits. • Identify trends in market pricing to make informed consumer choices. • Observe patterns in career earnings and financial growth over time. • Track fluctuations in financial markets and economic cycles. Scale, Proportion, and Quantity: • Compare salaries and cost-of-living differences in various career fields. • Analyze proportional budgeting to distribute income efficiently. • Apply mathematical calculations to determine interest rates and loan repayments. Cause and Effect: • Examine how financial decisions impact long-term wealth and stability. • Analyze the consequences of overspending and mismanagement of credit. • Understand how different saving strategies affect financial growth.
Social Emotional Learning (how it feels) Engage children in exploration of financial literacy & career readiness through hands-on projects on earning, saving, budgeting, & smart spending.		

Foundational STEM Coaching Resources

Please use the STEM For Kids® **The STEM Coaching Manual** as the foundational resource for how to bring STEM education to the students in your classroom.

Here is a list of common topics from **The STEM Coaching Manual** for your reference. These are subject to change. Kindly refer to the Manual for the latest:

<table>
<tr>
<td>

- **Foundations of STEM Coaching**
  - About STEM For Kids
  - The STEM Way

</td>
<td>

- **STEM For Kids 4 Dimensional Learning**
  - What it is
  - Career Connections & Practices
  - Cross-Cutting Concepts

</td>
</tr>
<tr>
<td>

- **Planning and Preparation**
  - Five Key Points of STEM Coaching
  - Course Training
  - Classroom Management
  - Frequently Asked Questions

- **Student Project Evaluation and Success**
  - Assessment Reports
    - Engineering Design Project Assessment
    - Teamwork Assessment
    - Social Emotional Learning Assessment
  - Student Peer Review
  - Pre- and Post- Attitude Surveys
  - Certificate of Completion

</td>
<td>

- **Conducting the Program**
  - Checklists & Responsibilities
    - First Day
    - Conducting Activities During A Class
    - Middle of Program
    - End of Program
  - Setting Children's Expectations
  - Accentuating Key Learnings
  - Customizing Program Delivery
  - Scaling Up or Down Activities
  - Parental/Community Engagement & Communications
  - Specific Activities for First Day, During the Program, and Last Day

</td>
</tr>
</table>

Important Guidelines for Delivering the Curriculum:

- Keep it fun and feel free to get into the fun yourself.
- Be a coach: enquire about children's thinking and encourage them to think in new ways.
- Listen for ideas from children.
- Encourage everyone's participation. Use children volunteers when you can.
- Start each day with a playful way to recap what children did previously (ideas are provided in the Ways to Recap section).
- End each day with a recap of main themes from the day.
- Use simple, age appropriate, language for describing the complex science and engineering concepts (each activity module provides you with guidelines and recommended way to approach a concept)
- Make kids curious and tap into that curiosity for maximum learning impact. Use best practices provided here and in the STEM Coaching Manual to arouse curiosity.

Any media (video and pictures) referenced throughout this book are provided in the STEM For Kids' STEM Coaches Member Area. For more information about membership and a free sampling of some of the available resources, visit **https://teach4d.stemforkids.net/start-free**.

The worksheets referenced throughout this instructional manual are available in the STEM For Kids® **Money Smart Kids: Building Financial Foundations Student's Workbook.**

Beginning the Program

At the beginning of each program, it is important that you outline the program expectations and how you expect participants to act throughout the various activities. Part of this beginning process involves having children introduce themselves in a fun, camp-like manner. Expectations will differ from program to program; however introductions, warm-up activities, and ice-breakers should be a part of a program's first day. This section will give you some ideas for how to do that. You are not limited to these activities.

Here are some common Beginning the Program Checklist items from **The STEM Coaching Manual**

Step 0	(Optional) Before the program starts, send a communique to the parents to set learning expectations and any needed logistical information.
Step 1	Complete the Walk-in and Drop Off procedures. Note and complete any additional procedures for the site.
Step 2	Complete the Pre-Assessment Attitude Survey with the participants.
Step 3	Pick one or two Introduction Games to conduct with the participants.
Step 4	Discuss the participant Expectations, Rewards and Consequences. Recall the 5 key points of STEM Coaching.
Step 5	(Optional) Conduct a Warm-Up Activity on the first day or any time children need to re-charge / re-focus.
Step 6	Conduct Internet Safety activities when working with the internet in a program.
Step 7	Do the Conducting Activities During a Class checklist throughout the day as you are going through your activities with the children.
Step 8	Leverage the STEM For Kids 4 Dimensional Learning Methodology by fostering Career Connections & Practices (CCPs) and exploring Cross-Cutting Concepts (CCCs) to inspire innovative thinking. Enquire about their thought processes, challenge them to consider new perspectives, and connect their learning to real-world applications and careers.
Step 9	Have fun! Allow the children to explore and learn in a low stress environment. Take pictures and videos throughout the day of the participants and full group, if applicable.
Step 10	RECAP RECAP RECAP. Complete Recap games throughout the day to promote key learning.
Step 11	Complete the Pick-Up and Location Close Out procedures per Daily Checklist. Note and complete any site specific procedures. Complete first day of program parent communique.

During the Program

During each program, it is essential to revisit and reinforce previously learned material to ensure long-term retention and deeper understanding. Regular review sessions help students connect new concepts with prior knowledge, fostering a stronger foundation for future learning. **The STEM Coaching Manual** offers a variety of engaging strategies and activities to facilitate this process, from interactive discussions to hands-on games.

However, feel free to adapt or introduce new methods that best suit the needs and dynamics of your students. The goal is to create meaningful opportunities for reflection and application, enhancing both confidence and competence as students progress through the program.

Here are some common During the Program Checklist items from **The STEM Coaching Manual**.

Step 1	Complete the Walk-in and Drop Off procedures. Note and complete any additional procedures for the site.
Step 2	Discuss the participant Expectations, Rewards and Consequences. Recall the 5 key points of STEM Coaching.
Step 3	(Optional) Conduct a Warm-Up Activity any time energy needs to be released.
Step 4	RECAP RECAP RECAP. Complete Recap games at the beginning of the day based on what concepts they learned the day before and on previous days.
Step 5	Do the Conducting Activities During a Class checklist throughout the day as you are going through your activities with the children.
Step 6	Leverage the STEM For Kids 4 Dimensional Learning Methodology by fostering Career Connections & Practices (CCPs) and exploring Cross-Cutting Concepts (CCCs) to inspire innovative thinking. Enquire about their thought processes, challenge them to consider new perspectives, and connect their learning to real-world applications and careers.
Step 7	Have fun! Allow the children to explore and learn in a low stress environment. Take pictures and videos throughout the day of the participants and full group, if applicable.
Step 8	RECAP RECAP RECAP. Complete Recap games at the end of the day based on what concepts they learned that day and on previous days.
Step 9	Complete the Pick-Up and Location Close Out procedures per Daily Checklist. Note and complete any site specific procedures. Complete middle of program parent communique.

Ending the Program

As the program concludes, it's important to celebrate achievements and reinforce learning through reflection, feedback, and recognition. Encourage participants to share their experiences and showcase their work to build confidence and strengthen their understanding. Incorporate activities that review key concepts, promote collaboration, and gather valuable insights on their growth. Providing opportunities for recognition and personal expression ensures a meaningful and lasting impact as participants complete the program.

Here are some common Ending the Program Checklist items from **The STEM Coaching Manual**.

Step 1	Complete the Walk-in and Drop Off procedures. Note and complete any additional procedures for the site.
Step 2	Discuss the participant Expectations, Rewards and Consequences. Recall the 5 key points of STEM Coaching.
Step 3	Use the During the Program Checklist.
Step 4	Have the participants show and tell the learning & projects they did in the program to parents and others.
Step 5	Complete the Post-Assessment Survey with the participants. Conduct Peer Feedback, Completion of Course Certificate, and Camper's Talk with the participants.
Step 6	RECAP RECAP RECAP. Complete Recap games at the end of the day based on what concepts they learned throughout the week.
Step 7	Complete the Pick-Up and Location Close Out procedures per Daily Checklist. Note and complete any site specific procedures. Complete last day parent communique.

STEM for kids

PATENT NO. _______

INVENTOR NAME(S): ____________________

____

INVENTION DATE: ____________________

UNIQUE DESIGN QUALITIES PATENTED:

SIGNATURE OF INVENTOR(S): ____________________

____

SIGNATURE OF ISSUER: ____________________

STEM for kids

PATENT NO. _______

INVENTOR NAME(S): ____________________

____

INVENTION DATE: ____________________

UNIQUE DESIGN QUALITIES PATENTED:

SIGNATURE OF INVENTOR(S): ____________________

____

SIGNATURE OF ISSUER: ____________________

STEMtastic Projects Registration Office

The undersigned hereby submit these Articles of Organization for the purpose of working together as a team in a class project.

The name of the company is: ________________________________

The project that we will do together is: ________________________________

____

____

____

The company will automatically dissolve at the completion of the project activity.

The name and role of each person completing this Articles of Organization is as follows (list every team member's first name and their role):

First Name Only	Role

These articles will be effective upon filing.

Today is the ________________ **day of** ____________________, ____________.
(number of the day) *(name of the month)* *(year)*

Engineers Talk
STEM for kids

Engineering Design Project Assessment

Use the provided Engineering Design Project Rubric to assess student understanding of the project or to grade the project for classroom usage.

Project Name:

	1 (Does Not Meet Expectations)	2 (Approaches Expectations)	3 (Meets Expectations)	4 (Exceeds Expectations)	Score (Out of 4)
Critical Thinking	Does not identify the problem or constraints.	Has difficulty identifying the problem or constraints.	Identifies the problem and some constraints.	Clearly identifies the problem and constraints.	
Design Process	Does not follow the design process.	Struggles to follow the design process.	Follows the design process with some gaps.	Follows the design process (ask, imagine, plan, create, improve) effectively.	
Creativity	Design is unoriginal and lacks creativity.	Design lacks creativity.	Demonstrates some creativity in the design.	Demonstrates a high level of creativity in the design.	
Functionality	The project does not meet the basic requirements of the challenge.	Project is not functionally sound.	Project is functionally sound but may have minor flaws.	Project is functionally sound and meets all the requirements of the challenge.	
Efficiency	Project is extremely inefficient in terms of materials and time.	Project is inefficient in terms of materials or time.	Project is reasonably efficient in terms of materials and time.	Project is efficient in terms of materials used and creation time.	
Presentation	Does not present the design process, results, and conclusions.	Struggles to present the design process, results, and conclusions.	Presents the design process, results, and conclusions with some clarity.	Clearly and effectively presents the design process, results, and conclusions.	

Feedback:

Total Score:

Teamwork Assessment

Use the provided Teamwork Rubric to assess student understanding of the project or to grade the project for classroom usage.

Project Name:

	1 (Does Not Meet Expectations)	2 (Approaches Expectations)	3 (Meets Expectations)	4 (Exceeds Expectations)	Score (Out of 4)
Active Participation	Rarely participates in team activities or contributes to discussions.	Participates in some team activities, but may be passive or disengaged.	Contributes to team discussions and decision-making, but may be less assertive.	Actively participates in all team discussions and decision-making processes.	
Effective Communication	Rarely communicates with team members or struggles to express ideas clearly.	Communicates with team members, but may have difficulty expressing ideas or listening to others.	Communicates effectively with team members, but may have occasional misunderstandings.	Communicates clearly and effectively with team members, both verbally and in writing.	
Conflict Resolution	Avoids conflict or escalates conflicts in a destructive manner.	May struggle to resolve conflicts or may resort to passive-aggressive behavior.	Handles conflicts respectfully and attempts to find compromises.	Actively seeks to resolve conflicts peacefully and collaboratively.	
Respect for Others	Disregards the opinions and contributions of others.	May be dismissive of others' ideas or contributions.	Generally respects others, but may have occasional disagreements.	Demonstrates respect for the ideas, opinions, and contributions of all team members.	
Teamwork	Rarely works collaboratively or undermines the team's efforts.	May have difficulty working collaboratively or may hinder the team's progress.	Contributes to the team's success, but may not always be fully engaged.	Works effectively as part of a team to achieve common goals.	
Shared Responsibility	Does not contribute to the team's workload and avoids taking responsibility.	May avoid taking responsibility or may contribute unequally to the team's workload.	Contributes to the team's workload, but may rely on others for support.	Takes ownership of their responsibilities and contributes equally to the team's workload.	

Feedback:

Total Score:

Social Emotional Learning Assessment

Use the provided Social Emotional Learning Rubric to evaluate and support the development of participants' social & emotional skills in the program.

Project Name:

	1 (Does Not Meet Expectations)	2 (Approaches Expectations)	3 (Meets Expectations)	4 (Exceeds Expectations)	Score (Out of 4)
Persistence	Shows little effort or persistence in completing the project.	May give up easily when faced with difficulties.	Persists through challenges, but may require occasional encouragement.	Demonstrates a high level of persistence and resilience in overcoming challenges.	
Time Management	Consistently misses deadlines and fails to complete the project.	Struggles to manage time effectively and may miss deadlines.	Completes the project on time, but may have occasional delays.	Effectively manages time and resources to complete the project on schedule.	
Work Ethic	Consistently fails to meet expectations in terms of work ethic.	Lacks organization and attention to detail.	Demonstrates a good work ethic, but may have occasional lapses.	Exhibits a strong work ethic, including punctuality, organization, and attention to detail.	
Initiative	Shows little initiative or interest in the project.	Relies heavily on instructions and guidance from others.	Shows initiative and willingness to take on additional responsibilities.	Takes initiative and goes above and beyond the requirements of the project.	
Quality of Work	Produces work that is clearly below standard.	Produces work that is incomplete or contains errors.	Produces good-quality work that is generally accurate and complete.	Produces high-quality work that is accurate, complete, and well-presented.	

Feedback:

Total Score:

Engineering Design Project

The Engineering Design Project (EDP) we use in STEM For Kids programs are meant to mimic, to some extent, the above real-life RFP process and engineering design. Emphasize to children that this is a real process used by engineers when they create technologies.

Explain to participants the stages of the EDP:

- **Ask**: After establishing the goal, we ask questions to understand the goal, the criteria and constraints, and how we will test our solution.
  - Goal - every EDP should have a clear goal. Goals can be laid out as:
    - Simply, build something to apply the concepts being learned.
    - Or, more complex, build / design something to solve a problem. In this case, you can present a problem.
  - Criteria - what are the critical success factors that will determine if the goal has been met? How will these be tested / measured?
  - Constraints - Engineering involves working under constraints. These constraints can be regarding how much money is available, time and people. So, it is important for participants to understand these constraints and work under these conditions.

- **Imagine**: We think about possible solutions by brainstorming ideas, before we choose the best one.

- **Plan**: We draw diagrams for a solution, and decide what materials to use.

- **Create**: Follow your plan, create it, and test it.
- **Improve:** Does your solution work? If so, how can we make it better? If not, how can we improve it?

Notes

Module 1: Right on the Money

This module teaches participants the fundamentals of money, including its purpose, forms, and the importance of making smart financial choices such as saving, earning, and budgeting. Participants will analyze real-world spending decisions, differentiate between needs and wants, and explore various ways to earn money while considering risks and rewards.

Materials

Materials for Class:

- Laptop/Projector
- Whiteboard
- Scissors
- Crayons / Markers
- Tape / Masking Tape
- Pencil
- Glue Stick or glue
- Construction/Printer Paper
- Bowls
- Recycled materials like boxes, bottles, etc.
- Art Supplies like stickers, washy tape, stamps, pipe cleaners, pom poms, etc.

Materials for Each Child/Group:

- Cardstock
- Stamps
- Clay, optional
- Cardboard
- Aluminum Foil
- Paper Bill Pen
- Decorations like stickers, gems, glitter, etc.
- Computer per student, optional

1.1: What is Money?

Time Required	45 - 60 min
Group Sizes	1
Grade	K - 5
Materials Needed	
• Laptop / Projector • Pencils • Different Forms of Currency • Envelopes / Small Bags • Construction Paper • Cardstock • Printer Paper • Crayons / Markers • Stickers / Stamps • Clay, optional • Cardboard • Aluminum Foil • Scissors • Tape • Paper Bill Pen	

Learning Objectives

- Define Money and Its Purpose – Explain that money is used to buy things we need and want, and recognize its role in everyday life.
- Introduce Smart Money Choices – Explain that money is not just for spending but also for saving and earning, helping people make thoughtful financial decisions for the future.
- Identify Different Forms of Physical Money – Recognize that money can exist as cash (bills and coins) and understand how each is used in everyday transactions.
- Understand the Value of Money – Compare different denominations of money, practice making change, and understand why we need various amounts for different purchases.
- Explain How Money Is Made – Describe the process of how paper bills and coins are produced by the government, including designing, printing, and security measures.
- Understand the Role of Security Features – Identify special features like color-shifting ink, ridges on coins, and quality checks that prevent counterfeiting and ensure money is reliable.
- Apply the Engineering Design Process to design and create a classroom currency system, incorporating security features and STEM-related symbols.
- Demonstrate an understanding of money's purpose and security by designing durable, functional bills and coins with unique features to prevent counterfeiting.

Have the participants sit in a central location with a whiteboard/screen for a discussion about money. Begin by saying that money is an important part of everyday life. Ask the participants: What is money? See some answers below.

> *"It's what grown-ups use to buy stuff." "It's paper and coins that you use to buy toys and snacks." "It's something you keep in a piggy bank." "It's what the tooth fairy gives me." "It's what you get when you do chores." "It's what my grandma gives me on my birthday." "It's invisible when you use a card."*

On the whiteboard, write the following:

Money is something we use to buy things we need and want.

On the whiteboard, draw the following table. Ask the participants: What are some needs? What are some wants? Write out the answers in the correct columns. Once done, say, money helps people buy things they need (like food, clothes, and shelter) and things they want (like toys, games, and special treats).

What Are Some Needs?	What Are Some Wants?
"Food" "A house" "Clothes" "Water or Soda" "Electricity" "Gas" "Medicine" "School supplies like pencils and books" "Soap" "Paying for the doctor" "Shoes" "A phone" "Pet food"	"Toys" "Ice cream and candy" "Video games" "A teddy bear" "Going to Disneyland" "A skateboard" "Cool shoes with lights on them" "An iPad" "A trampoline" "Movie tickets and popcorn" "A bike" "Glittery stickers and fun markers" "Dress-up clothes and costumes"

Explain that money is not just about spending - It's also about saving, earning, and making smart choices. Understanding how money works helps people make good choices. Whether it's deciding between spending money on candy today or saving for a new bike later, learning about money helps us plan for a brighter future. We'll be going over these topics in this program to make sure we are smart about our money!

Money Match Up Game

Ask the participants: What does money look like?

> *"It's paper with numbers on it." "It's round and shiny like a coin." "It's green and crinkly." "It has pictures of important people on it." "It's a card my parents swipe at the store." "It's numbers on a screen when you pay with a phone." "It has numbers to tell you how much it's worth."*

Money comes in different forms. It can be cash (dollar bills and coins), digital money (used in apps and online banking), or credit and debit cards. While we may not always see money in our hands, we use it every day—when we buy groceries, pay for transportation, or even purchase things online.

Show participants different forms of currency from your country. For the purposes of this activity, we will talk about the USD, but all instructions can be used with your currency.

Place the different physical currencies on a table. Point at certain coins and ask questions like "How much is a nickel?" or "Which is worth more, a dime or a penny?" Let the participants know the amounts for each physical currency. Ask clarifying questions like "How many nickels are in a quarter?" or "If I gave you a $10 bill to break into $1 bills and $5 bills, what could you give me?"

Provide the following worksheet to practice simple currency math - Understand that the money discussed is generic but can be applied to real world currency.

Once completed with the discussion / worksheet, ask: Why do we need different amounts of money?

> *"Because not everything costs the same" "So we don't have to carry a bag of coins" "Some things are cheap, and some things are expensive" "So stores can give us the right amount back when we pay"*

Tell the participants that we need different amounts of money because not everything costs the same. Some things, like a piece of candy, are cheap, while other things, like a bike or a house, cost a lot more. Having different coins and bills helps us pay the right amount for whatever we're buying. If we only had $100 bills, it would be really hard to buy something small, like a snack. Different amounts of money also help us save, make change, and buy both little and big things in the real world.

Money Matters

Part 1: Match the Cost!

Look at each item below and match it with the correct cost by drawing a line. Write out what bills or coins you would use to pay for that item.
(Example: If the cost is $17.00, write "One $10, One $5, Two $1")

A pack of gum	$12.00 ______________________
A bicycle	$40.00 ______________________
A toy car	$1.00 ______________________
A candy bar	$150.00 ______________________
A movie ticket	$2.25 ______________________
A video game	$8.00 ______________________

Part 2: Real-Life Purchase Decisions

Read the scenarios below and answer the questions. Think about how much money you have, how you would pay, and if you should save or spend!

You want to buy a toy car that costs $8. You have $10 in your pocket.

a. How much money will you have left after buying the toy?

____

b. What are the bills or coins you would receive?

____

You want to buy a movie ticket that costs $12, but you only have $8.

a. How much money do you need?

____

b. What could you do to get enough money to buy the movie ticket?

____

c. Would you save your money or try to get more?

____

You see a toy bike for $30. You have $25,

- Should you save your money for a bigger purchase or try to buy something else?

____

- What other items could you buy with $25?

____

Part 3: Save, Spend, or Share?

Read the situations below and decide if you should Save, Spend, or Share your money. Circle your answer.

1. You have $10, and you want a new game that costs $15.
   Save Spend Share
2. Your friend needs $2 for lunch, and you have $5.
   Save Spend Share
3. You have $5, and you see a cool toy for $4.
   Save Spend Share
4. You've saved $20, but you want to buy a fancy lunch for $18.
   Save Spend Share
5. You have $5, but you find a candy bar for $2 and a toy for $4.
   Save Spend Share
6. You want to buy a new video game for $25, but you only have $12.
   Save Spend Share
7. You want to buy a bicycle for $100, but you have $60.
   Save Spend Share
8. You have $30, & your friend is having a birthday party. The gift you want to buy costs $20.
   Save Spend Share
9. You find a $5 bill on the ground. What do you do with it?
   Save Spend Share
10. You have $10 and see a cute T-shirt for $8 and a toy for $6.
   Save Spend Share

Part 4: Spending Challenge!

Imagine you have $20. Write a plan for how you would use this $20.

1. What would you buy?

   ____

   ____

2. How much money would you save?

   ____

3. What could you share with others?

   ____

   ____

Hand out the cut out cards for the Money Match-Up game in an envelope to each participant. Make sure the cards are shuffled. Have the participants spread out the cards on the table or floor. Have them match the money card with the value or item card. Once finished, check their answers and provide a sticker if they get the answers correct!

Note to Coach: You can swap the money cards for play money or the print out money worksheet below. Print the worksheet multiple times to have a set of play money for the participants to use.

Extension - Team Play Option: Divide students into small teams and race to correctly match all money types with their corresponding values or items. Ask students to "buy" an item by choosing the correct amount of money.

Answers for the Money Match Up Game:

- Toy Car - $15.00
- Ice Cream Cone - $1.50
- Bicycle - $20.00
- Book - $5.00
- Candy Bar - $2.50
- Video Game - $15.00
- Movie Ticket - $12.00
- Pack of Stickers - $3.00
- T-shirt - $8.00
- Pizza Slice - $4.00

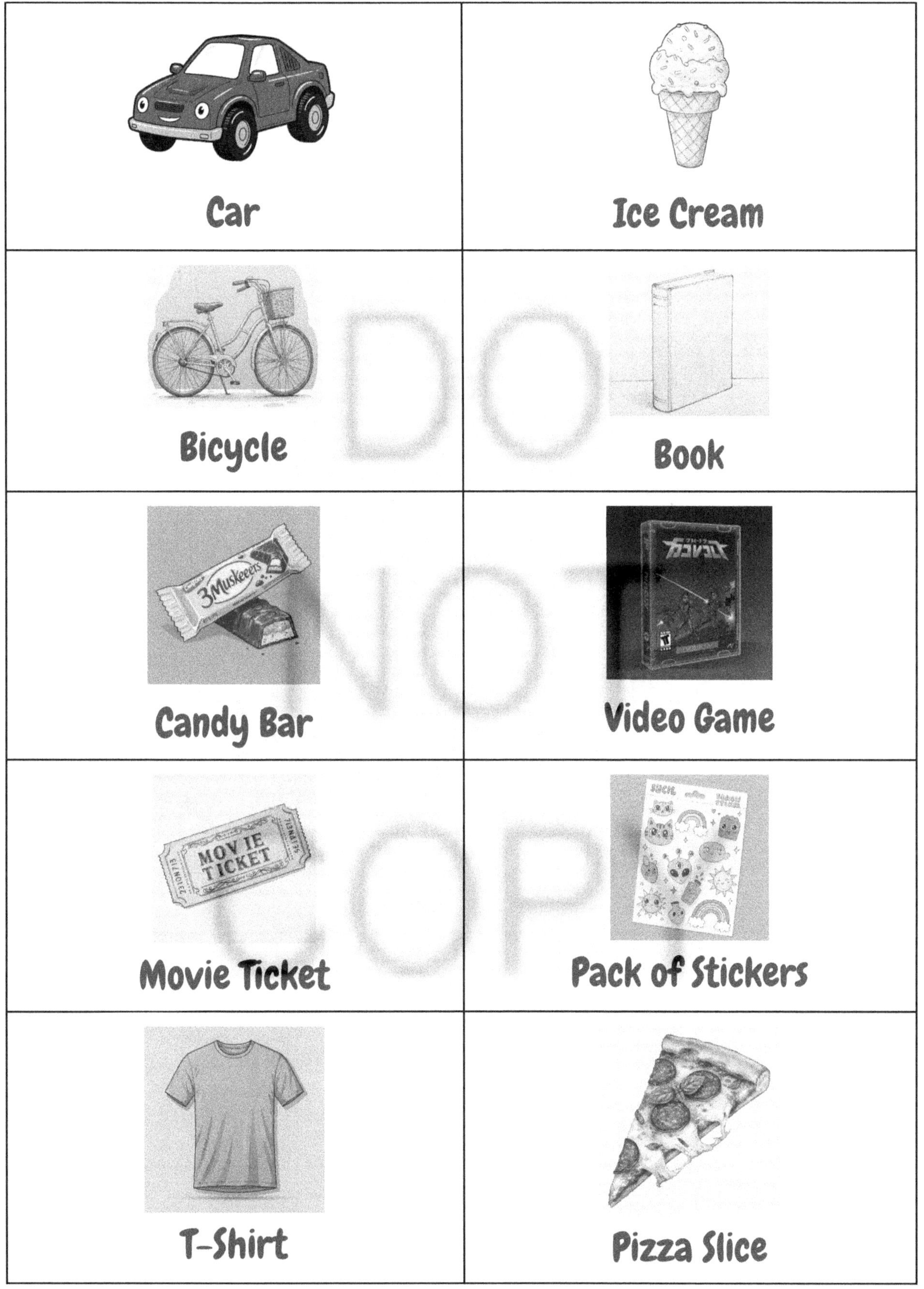
Car
Ice Cream
Bicycle
Book
3Muskeeers
Candy Bar
Video Game
MOV IE
TICKET
Movie Ticket
Pack of Stickers
T-Shirt
Pizza Slice

$1.50	$5.00
$10.00	$3.00
$20.00	$2.50
$15.00	$8.00
$12.00	$4.00

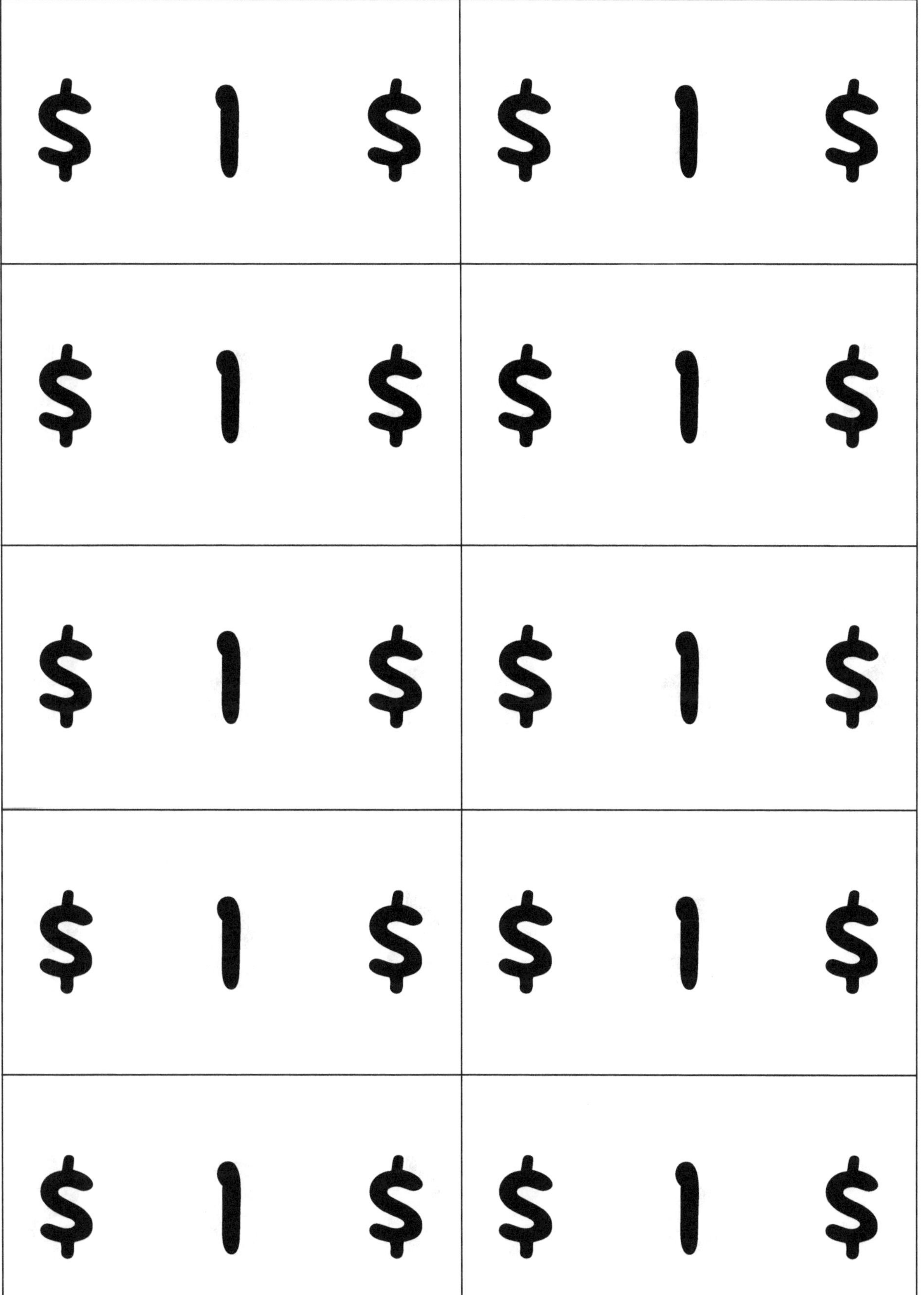
$ 1 $
$ 1 $
$ 1 $
$ 1 $
$ 1 $
$ 1 $
$ 1 $
$ 1 $
$ 1 $
$ 1 $

$ 5 $
$ 5 $
$ 5 $
$ 5 $
$ 5 $
$ 5 $
$ 5 $
$ 5 $
$ 5 $
$ 5 $

$ 10 $	$ 10 $
$ 10 $	$ 10 $
$ 10 $	$ 10 $
$ 10 $	$ 10 $
$ 10 $	$ 10 $

$ 20 $	$ 20 $
$ 20 $	$ 20 $
$ 20 $	$ 20 $
$ 20 $	$ 20 $
$ 20 $	$ 20 $

$ 50 $	$ 50 $
$ 50 $	$ 50 $
$ 50 $	$ 50 $
$ 50 $	$ 50 $
$ 50 $	$ 50 $

$ 100 $	$ 100 $
$ 100 $	$ 100 $
$ 100 $	$ 100 $
$ 100 $	$ 100 $
$ 100 $	$ 100 $

$ 0.01 $	$ 0.01 $
$ 0.01 $	$ 0.01 $
$ 0.01 $	$ 0.01 $
$ 0.01 $	$ 0.01 $
$ 0.01 $	$ 0.01 $

$ 0.05 $	$ 0.05 $
$ 0.05 $	$ 0.05 $
$ 0.05 $	$ 0.05 $
$ 0.05 $	$ 0.05 $
$ 0.05 $	$ 0.05 $

$ 0.10 $	$ 0.10 $
$ 0.10 $	$ 0.10 $
$ 0.10 $	$ 0.10 $
$ 0.10 $	$ 0.10 $
$ 0.10 $	$ 0.10 $

$ 0.25 $	$ 0.25 $
$ 0.25 $	$ 0.25 $
$ 0.25 $	$ 0.25 $
$ 0.25 $	$ 0.25 $
$ 0.25 $	$ 0.25 $

$ 0.50 $	$ 0.50 $
$ 0.50 $	$ 0.50 $
$ 0.50 $	$ 0.50 $
$ 0.50 $	$ 0.50 $
$ 0.50 $	$ 0.50 $

Where Does Money Come From? Discussion and Story

Ask the participants the following questions: Do you know where money comes from? How about how money is made? Can we make money at home and use it at a store?

Note to Coach: Do a little research on where your country's money is made to talk to the participants about the process. We will discuss the USD.

Explain that money is carefully made by the government to keep it safe, strong, and difficult to copy. In the United States, paper bills are made at the Bureau of Engraving and Printing, and coins are made at the U.S. Mint. Other countries have their own places where they make money.

Use the following story sheet to discuss where money is made in the United States. You can substitute certain spots with your country's currency information.

Once done reading the story, have the following discussion for paper bills and coins:

For Paper Bills:

1. **Designing:** Artists create detailed designs, including images of famous people and security features.
2. **Printing:** Special ink is used to print bills in layers, including color-shifting ink and hidden details. Paper bills are printed with special ink to make them more secure and harder to counterfeit (fake).
    a. Special inks, like color-shifting ink, help stop people from making fake money. When you tilt a real bill, the ink changes color! (Show money pen)
3. **Drying:** The ink dries for **three days** to prevent smudging.
4. **Cutting:** The large sheets of bills are cut into individual pieces.
5. **Checking for Mistakes:** Bills with errors are removed before being sent to banks.

For Coins:

1. **Melting Metal:** Coins are made from metals like copper, nickel, and zinc.
2. **Rolling and Cutting:** The metal is flattened into sheets and cut into circles.
3. **Stamping:** A machine stamps the design onto the coin.
4. **Edge Marking:** Some coins get special ridges on the sides to prevent people from shaving off metal.
5. **Polishing and Checking:** Coins are cleaned and checked before being sent to banks.

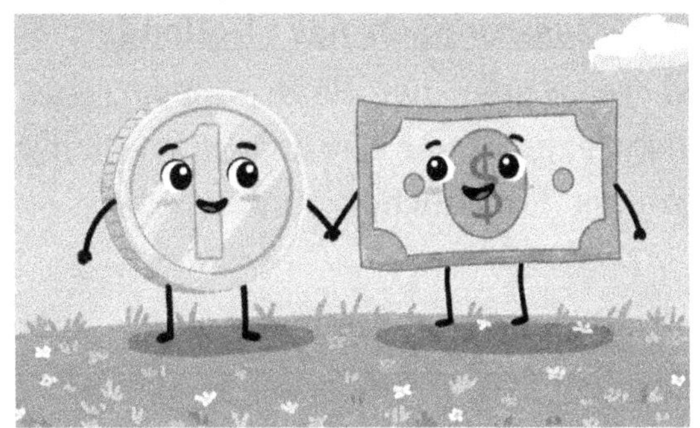

Penny the coin and Dollar the bill sat in a bank, waiting for their next adventure.

"Do you remember how we were made?" Penny asked.

"Of course!" Dollar said. "I was printed at the Bureau of Engraving and Printing! First, I was designed with special pictures, like the President's face and secret symbols to keep me safe."

"Wow!" Penny said. "I was made at the U.S. Mint. I started as a big sheet of metal that was flattened and cut into circles. Then, a machine stamped my design on both sides."

"That's so cool!" Dollar replied. "After I was printed, I had to dry for three days before being checked for mistakes. Then I was cut into rectangles and sent to banks!"

"And I got counted and polished before I was packed into rolls!" Penny added.

Just then, a bank teller picked them up and put them in a cash register.

"Time for a new adventure!" Dollar said.

Penny and Dollar couldn't wait to be spent!

Classroom Money Challenge

Participants will design and create their own classroom currency using STEM concepts. They will incorporate security features and key images on their classroom currency. Use the "Engineering Design Process" introduction on page 11.

Together as a class, decide on the currency name for the classroom. You can write suggestions on the whiteboard and call a vote for the name we will use in class going forward. Examples are "Class Bucks," "STEM Dollars," "Brain Coins," etc.

Decide on the values that you want to use in the classroom. We need different bill amounts (e.g. $1, $5, $10) and coin values (e.g. $0.10, $0.25). Write on the whiteboard what is decided and how many of each currency they need to create for classroom rewards.

Use the following Engineering Design Project description:

Goal: Make a set of classroom currency to use in class out of materials provided:

- Construction Paper
- Cardstock
- Printer Paper
- Crayons / Markers
- Stickers / Stamps
- Clay, optional
- Cardboard
- Aluminum Foil

Materials to help build but will not be used as part of your design.

- Tape, scissors

Explain when engineers work their supplies are limited, so they have to plan for a small amount of supplies.

Criteria:

- Each denomination of paper bill or coin should have a STEM-focused picture (e.g. a classroom mascot, famous scientist, symbol for each letter in STEM, etc.)

- The paper bills must have the following security features:
    - Hidden symbols (a tiny word or design that is hard to see)
        - Can be decided together as a class

  - Color-changing effect (use two colors on the words that look blended)
  - Serial numbers (each bill should have a different number)

- The coins must have ridges.

Constraints

- Use only the materials as specified.
- Each symbol should be unique to that currency denomination.
- The coins must have a certain size for each denomination and be consistent.
- The paper bills must have the correct image for each denomination and be consistent.

Test

- See if the materials stay together.
- Check durability of placing the currency in your pocket, bag, folder, etc.
- Do a security check by swapping money with a classmate and have them try to spot the security features.

Use the "My Engineering and Design Process" worksheets.

During class, allow the participants to use their classroom currency to "buy" small rewards as they complete projects (stickers, extra recess, classroom privileges).

My Engineering Design Process

Did it work?
YES: How can it be better?
NO: How can we fix it?

What do we have to work with and what do we want it to do?

Improve

Ask

The Goal:

What have we learned to complete this challenge?

Create

Imagine

Build it!

Plan

Draw out a few ideas on how to complete this challenge:

My Engineering Design Plan

Material	Properties	How could you use it in your design?

Draw a possible solution:

1.2 Importance of Finance

Time Required	30 min
Group Sizes	1 - 3
Grade	3 - 8
Materials Needed	
• Laptop / Projector • Whiteboard / Markers	

Learning Objective

- Understand the Basics of Finance – Participants will learn that finance involves managing money, including earning, spending, and saving, with a focus on personal finance and budgeting.
- Compare Different Types of Finance – Participants will explore how finance works at home, in schools, and within the government, recognizing the importance of budgeting and prioritizing expenses.
- Analyze Budgeting and Spending – Participants will review budget examples, identify differences between planned and actual expenses, and discuss strategies for managing surplus or unexpected costs.

Ask the participants if they know what finance is. Finance involves the management of money. This is especially so for governments or large companies. Finance must have money in order to exist. Money can be earned, spent, and saved.

For this curriculum, we are mostly going to look at personal finance. We will discover what we can do with money, the differences between needs and wants, and why budgeting keeps us from uncontrolled spending.

There are several finance examples as money is a large part of everything. We are going to look at 3 examples of finance: Home, School, and Government.

Home Finance

Home finance has to do with personal expenses within a family. Have the participants write on the whiteboard what they might expect to spend money on at home.
Housing/rent, water, food, electricity, fun days out, classes, etc.

Many people set budgets for themselves to keep track of personal expenses. They know how much money they have coming in from their job and can see how much money they may have available to use after their standard expenses.

Show the participants the following budget example of one person.

Category	Monthly Budget Amount	Actual Amount	Difference
Amount Earned:	$872	$810	$62
Expenses:			
Rent / Mortgage	$298	$239	$59
Utilities	$99	$120	$4
Groceries / Food	$121	$100	$21
Clothing	$66	$60	$6
Shopping	$55	$46	$9
Entertainment	$44	$44	$0
Miscellaneous / Other	$35	$31	$4
Expenses Subtotal	$718	$640	$78
Net Income (Income – Expenses)	$154	$170	

Ask the participants what they notice about the budget this person set for themselves. Are there any expenses that were much different than what was budgeted for? What do you suggest this person do with the extra money they had at the end of the month?

School Finance

Another finance example is a school budget. A budget in a school system refers to how the district uses its funds. Some departments will get more money than others due to the money being prioritized. A lot of the budget is tied to personnel and benefits. Having a budget allows school districts to justify the collection and use of public funds.

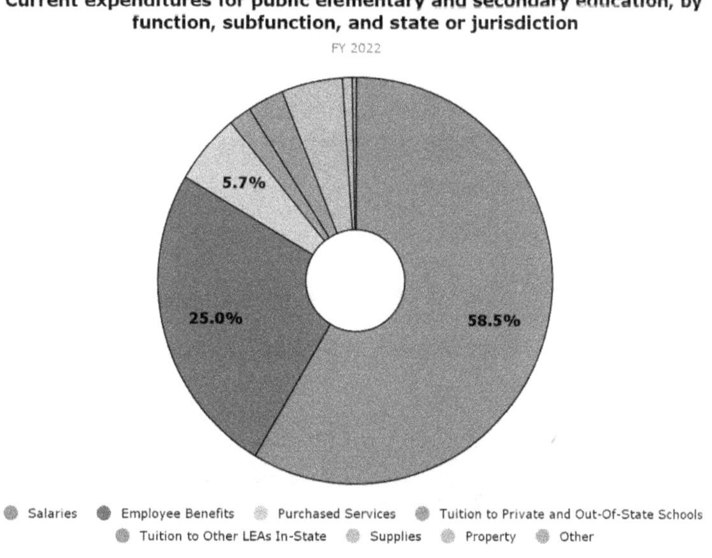

Cornman, S.Q., Doyle, S., Moore, C., Phillips, J., and Nelson, M.R. (2024). Revenues and Expenditures for Public Elementary and Secondary Education: School Year 2021–22 (Fiscal Year 2022): First Look (NCES 2024-301). U.S. Department of Education. Washington, DC: National Center for Education Statistics. Retrieved 3/2025 from http://nces.ed.gov/pubsearch .

School budget resources come from a combination of local, state, and federal contributions. The funds are spent continuously throughout the year. The major budget categories are transportation, facilities, energy, health and safety, instruction, curriculum and staff development, food services, library services, counseling services, and school leadership and support.

Show the participants the following example graph of where the school funding goes. There is more to a school budget than what is listed in the table.

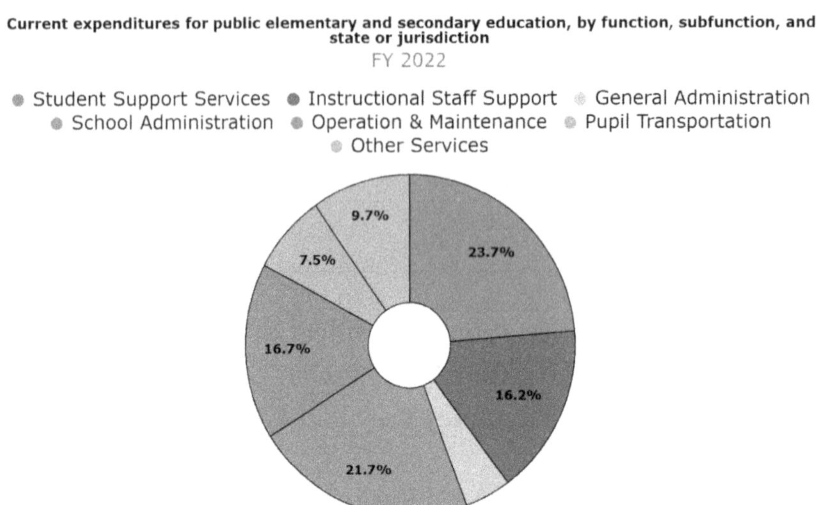

Cornman, S.Q., Doyle, S., Moore, C., Phillips, J., and Nelson, M.R. (2024). Revenues and Expenditures for Public Elementary and Secondary Education: School Year 2021–22 (Fiscal Year 2022): First Look (NCES 2024-301). U.S. Department of Education. Washington, DC: National Center for Education Statistics. Retrieved 3/2025 from http://nces.ed.gov/pubsearch.

Government Finance

The final example of finance refers to the government. The U.S. Treasury divides all federal spending into three groups: mandatory spending, discretionary spending, and interest on debt.

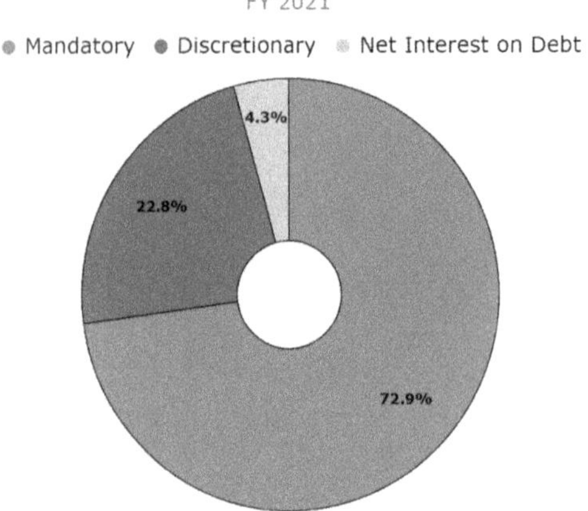

Source: OMB (https://www.whitehouse.gov/omb/), National Priorities Project (https://www.nationalpriorities.org/budget-basics/federal-budget-101/spending/)

Mandatory and discretionary spending accounts for 95.7% of all federal spending and pays for all government services and programs which we rely on.

Discretionary spending refers to a number of departments from military to energy to education. More than half of the discretionary spending is sent to the military.

Federal Discretionary Spending

FY 2021

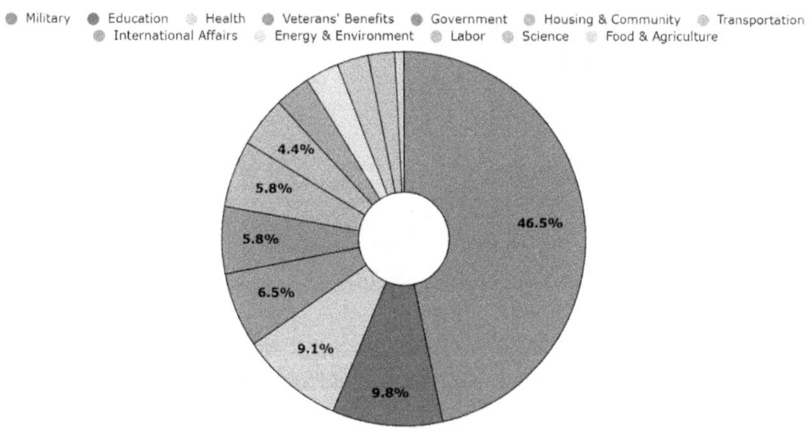

Source: OMB (https://www.whitehouse.gov/omb/), National Priorities Project (https://www.nationalpriorities.org/budget-basics/federal-budget-101/spending/)

Mandatory spending refers to departments that must have a certain amount of money every year. These departments are mostly benefit programs.

Federal Mandatory Spending

FY 2021

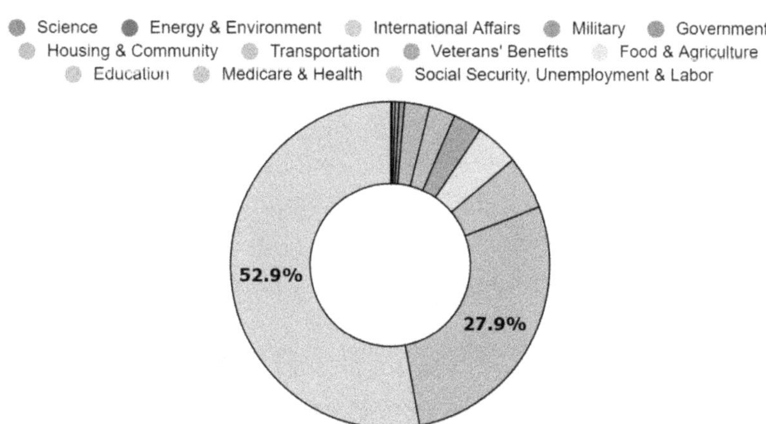

Source: OMB (https://www.whitehouse.gov/omb/), National Priorities Project (https://www.nationalpriorities.org/budget-basics/federal-budget-101/spending/)

Interest on debt refers to the interest the government pays on its own debt. See the graph below for the total federal spending.

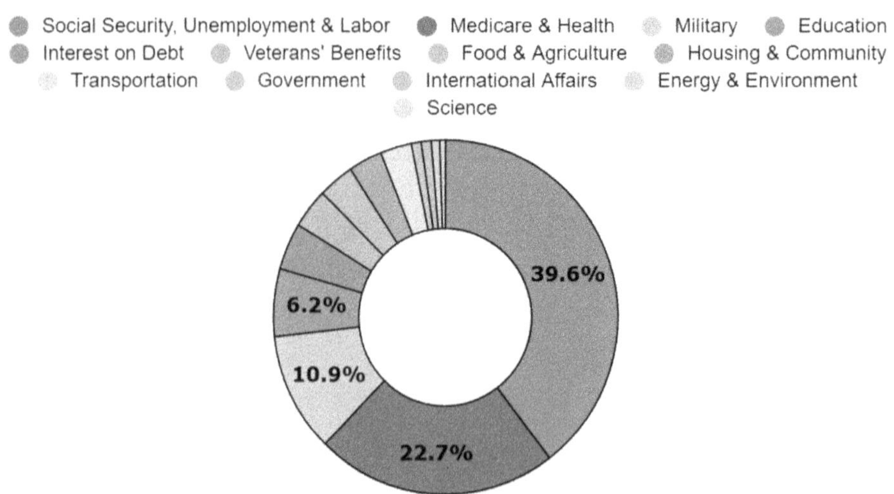

Source: OMB (https://www.whitehouse.gov/omb/), National Priorities Project (https://www.nationalpriorities.org/budget-basics/federal-budget-101/spending/)

Tax breaks, also known as "tax expenditures," are a form of government spending where lawmakers have created incentives within the federal tax code. Examples include special tax rates on investments and deductions for home mortgage interest. In 2020, these tax breaks cost the federal government over $1.3 trillion, almost the same amount as all discretionary spending for that year. Unlike typical government spending, tax breaks reduce the amount of tax revenue collected, essentially functioning as a form of indirect spending.

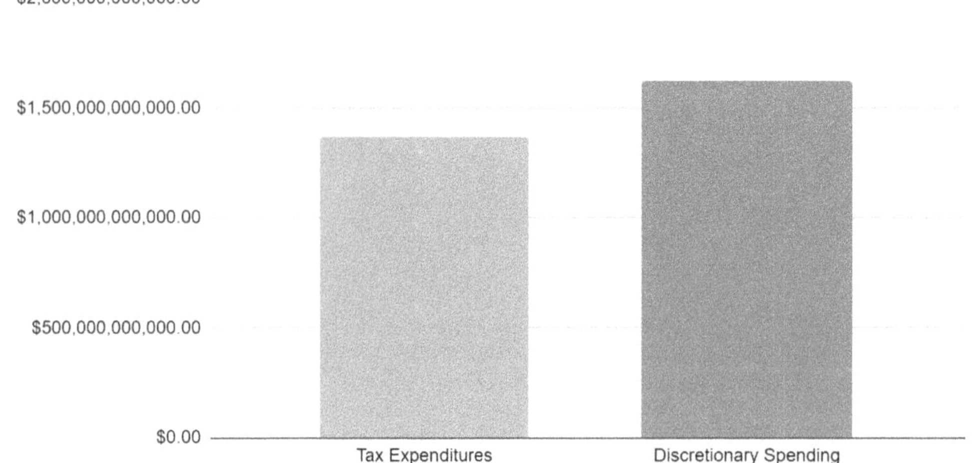

Source: OMB (https://www.whitehouse.gov/omb/), National Priorities Project (https://www.nationalpriorities.org/budget-basics/federal-budget-101/spending/)

1.3 Money Money Money

Time Required	30 min
Group Sizes	1 - 3
Grade	K - 8
Materials Needed	
• Laptop/Projector • Whiteboard/Marker	

Learning Objective

- Identify Ways to Earn Money – Participants will explore different methods of earning money, including working a job, selling products, and providing services.
- Evaluate Risks and Rewards of Earning Money – Participants will analyze various ways to earn money, considering the potential benefits and challenges associated with each method.
- Develop Critical Thinking and Decision-Making Skills – Participants will collaborate in groups to discuss and determine the most effective ways to earn money based on their ideas and insights.

Explain to the participants that we are going to first look at how we can earn money. Without earning money, we will not have money to spend!

Have the participants write on the whiteboard ways that they can earn money. *Getting a job, selling something, providing a service.*

When participants get a job to earn money, they work at a certain company to complete responsibilities that the company needs done in order to survive. Ask what type of job their parents, siblings, or even grandparents have. How are they giving back to the company they work for? They are doing something for that company in order to earn money.

Participants can also earn money by selling something. There are a lot of websites that allow people to sell a product that they made, found, or had. Can the participants think of a few websites that allow people to sell products? *eBay, Amazon, Craigslist, Etsy, etc.* They may also have their own store and sell products there as well.

Lastly, participants can earn money by providing a service. They can tutor someone chemistry, babysit for a family, or even mow lawns. A service may not always be needed.

Hand each participant the worksheet below. Explain that they are going to come up with 6 ways that they can earn money. They will also think of the risks and rewards for earning money that way.

For example, one way could be raking leaves for their neighbors. A reward would be earning money as well as helping their neighbors that may be elderly or work all day. A risk would be that normally raking leaves is only done in the autumn.

Once finished with the worksheet, have everyone get into groups of 3 and discuss the 6 ways they wrote down. Have them pick the best 2 ways and write them on the whiteboard.

6 Ways to Earn Money

Write out the 6 ways you can earn money. Make sure to fill out the rewards and risks on earning money that way.

Way #1:

Rewards:

Risks:

Way #2:

Rewards:

Risks:

Way #3:

Rewards:

Risks:

Way #4:

Rewards:

Risks:

Way #5:

Rewards:

Risks:

Way #6:

Rewards:

Risks:

1.4 Money Spent

<table>
<tr><td>Time Required</td><td>30 - 45 mins</td></tr>
<tr><td>Group Sizes</td><td>1</td></tr>
<tr><td>Grade</td><td>K - 5</td></tr>
<tr><td colspan="2">Materials Needed</td></tr>
<tr><td colspan="2"><ul><li>Laptop/Projector</li><li>Whiteboard/Marker</li><li>Bowls</li><li>Fake Money, optional</li><li>Computer per student, optional</li><li>Paper / Crayons / Markers / Stickers</li></ul></td></tr>
</table>

Learning Objective

- Differentiate Between Needs and Wants:Participants will be able to define and categorize purchases as either needs (essential expenses) or wants (non-essential purchases).
- Analyze Spending Decisions: Participants will evaluate real-life spending scenarios, justify their choices, and discuss the impact of prioritizing needs over wants.
- Apply Smart Shopping Strategies: Participants will explore and demonstrate strategies for making wise financial decisions, including budgeting, price comparison, and prioritizing essential purchases.

As people spend money, they usually have a budget of things that they want or need. Every purchase falls into one of these two categories: A want or a need. A want refers to a purchase that a person wants to have but can wait. A need is a purchase that must be done and cannot wait.

Some need purchases refer to rent of a house, food, a car payment, or even an emergency purchase. Some want purchases may refer to fun nights out, new shoes, or a candy bar. Sometimes, knowing which category a purchase falls under can be hard to distinguish.

Needs VS Wants Physical Game

Let the participants know that we are going to play a game. We are going to decide if a purchase is a need or a want. Have the participants stand on one side of the room. If they decide it is a need, they will sit on the floor. If they decide it is a want, they will stay standing. If they get the correct answer, then they will take one step forward. If the answer they provided is wrong, they will stay where they are.

The STEM Coach will stand on the other side of the room and tell the participants scenarios. Once a participant reaches the other end of the room from the start point, they win the game!

Here are the scenarios for the participants to decide if the purchase is a need or a want. You may come up with your own as well.

- Stacey bought $100 shoes because her friend has a pair.
- James paid for a $50 electricity bill.
- Pat bought a $10 shirt because she needed a shirt for work.
- Nate bought 4 2-litter drinks for the month.
- Jenny bought a new car.
- Yuri bought a ring for her mom.
- Tiara decided to buy lunch for a friend who didn't have enough money.

Needs VS Wants Sorting Game

Let the participants know that we are going to play a game. We are going to decide if a purchase is a need or a want. Participants will learn the difference between needs and wants by sorting various items into the correct category and discussing why each item fits.

Hand out the "Needs VS Wants" cards to each participant. Place two bowls at the front of the room - One bowl titled "Needs" and another bowl titled "Wants." One at a time, participants will take turns placing their card in either the "Needs" or "Wants" bowl.

After each placement, ask the group and have a productive discussion:

- Do you agree? Why or why not?
- Could this item sometimes be both?
  (e.g., shoes are a need, but designer sneakers might be a want).

Extension - Budgeting Challenge: Give participants a set amount of fake money (e.g. $20) - See Module 1 Activity 1 for printable fake money. On the whiteboard, tape the "Needs VS Wants" cards so that participants can view what options are available. Ask them to "spend" their money wisely.

Afterwards, ask the group and have a productive discussion:

- Did you prioritize needs first?
- What did you have to give up?
- How did you feel about your choices?

You ran out of toothpaste. **Toothbrush & Toothpaste** **$5.00**	You ran out of personal hygiene. **Soap & Shampoo** **$5.00**
You see a new shirt. **Shirt** **$10.00**	You are hungry. **Sandwich** **$5.00**
Your shoes fell apart. **Shoes** **$15.00**	You're not feeling well. **Medicine** **$5.00**
Your class requires a notebook. **Notebook** **$2.00**	Your class requires a pencil. **Pencils** **$2.00**
You are going to school by Uber. **Transportation** **$10.00**	You cannot see. **Glasses** **$100.00**
You are cold outside. **Winter Coat** **$50.00**	You require a uniform for school. **School Uniform** **$30.00**
You see a candy bar. **Candy Bar** **$1.50**	You see a new video game. **Video Game** **$60.00**
You are at the fast food joint. **Chicken Nuggets** **$5.00**	You are at the store. **Stuffed Animal** **$10.00**
You are watching TV. **TV Streaming Service** **$15.00**	Your favorite artist is in town. **Concert Ticket** **$50.00**
You see a new interesting movie. **Movie Ticket** **$12.00**	You see a building set at the store. **Building Toy Set** **$70.00**
Your tablet just broke. **Tablet** **$250.00**	You are invited to go on a bike ride. **Bicycle** **$150.00**
You are going on vacation. **Trip to Amusement Park** **$200.00**	You are decorating a project. **Stickers** **$1.00**

1.5 Penny Saved is a Penny Earned

Time Required	45 - 60 mins
Group Sizes	1
Grade	K - 5
Materials Needed	
• Whiteboard / Marker • Recycled materials like boxes, bottles, etc. • Art Supplies like stickers, washy tape, stamps, pipe cleaners, pom poms, etc. • Scissors • Tape • Crayons / Markers	

Learning Objective

- Understand what saving money means and how to use the money saved proactively.
- Design and build a piggy bank with recycled materials to begin a savings fund at home.
- Understand the application of the engineering design process to certain goals, criteria, and constraints.
- Design and build a piggy bank while adhering to specified criteria, including using at least four different materials and staying within the provided resources.
- Understand the importance of planning and optimizing limited resources, similar to real-world engineering projects.

Ask the participants if they know what a savings is. Explain that their parents will more than likely have savings. A savings is the result of putting money in a separate bank account to use at a later date. Instead of spending money immediately as you get it, you can be money smart and save it for later.

Have the participants brainstorm why they may want to save their money instead of spending it. Have them come up to the whiteboard and write their answers. *Can buy little things later like a snack or movie trip, can save up for a big item for themselves or others, use for emergencies such as a jacket that was lost or a lock for their bike.*

Explain that, once the participants have saved enough money, they may want to put their money into a savings account at a bank. Ask if anyone has heard of or been to a bank before. Banks keep your money safe. When you give your money to a bank, it is called a deposit.

<u>Piggy Bank Engineering Design Challenge</u>

Tell the participants that we will be using the EDP to design, build, and improve a piggy bank that they can use at home and in class.

Goal: Make a piggy bank using **<u>at least 4</u>** different materials provided.

Materials Provided:

- Recycled materials like boxes, bottles, etc.
- Art Supplies like stickers, washy tape, stamps, pipe cleaners, pom poms, etc.
- Scissors
- Tape
- Crayons / Markers

Explain when engineers work, their supplies are limited, so they have to plan their designs taking into account the small amount of supplies available. Common materials like markers, crayons, glue, scissors, etc are available.

Criteria:

- The piggy bank must be able to securely hold coins and/or paper money. It should have a slot for inserting money. The design should include a way to retrieve the money without breaking the bank.

- The piggy bank should have a unique or creative design (e.g., themed, colorful, animal-shaped, futuristic).

- The piggy bank should be sturdy enough to hold money without tipping over or breaking easily.

Constraints: Use only the materials provided. Use at least 4 different materials.

Test: Test by making sure you can place your classroom money in the piggy bank.

My Engineering Design Process

Did it work?
YES: How can it be better?
NO: How can we fix it?

What do we have to work with and what do we want it to do?

Improve

Ask

The Goal:

What have we learned to complete this challenge?

Create

Imagine

Build it!

Plan

Draw out a few ideas on how to complete this challenge:

My Engineering Design Plan

Material	Properties	How could you use it in your design?

Draw a possible solution:

1.6 Recap

Time Required	15 - 20 min
Group Sizes	1
Grade	K - 8
Materials Needed	
• Paper • Pencil • Whiteboard	

Learning Objective

- Recall and apply terms and ideas related to finance, money, and engineering through an interactive activity.
- Provide an informal opportunity to evaluate participants' comprehension of key topics covered in class.
- Develop the ability to convey and recognize ideas through drawing and verbal explanation.
- Build teamwork and camaraderie by encouraging participants to work together during the game.

Play a game of Pictionary. Have a participant go to the board and begin to draw a picture. Other participants can then guess what they think is being drawn. The participant to guess correctly is next to draw.

Use words and objects that we have been talking about in class.

Examples of words that can be used:

- Finance
- Money
- Needs
- Wants
- Coins
- Paper Bills
- Piggy Bank
- Engineering
- Building
- Planning
- Testing

Notes

Module 2: Smart Shoppers

This module teaches participants how to save money using coupons, compare prices, and make smart financial decisions while practicing budgeting and math skills. Through hands-on activities, they will explore different payment methods, develop critical thinking, and learn responsible money management for real-life shopping scenarios.

Materials

Materials for the Class:

- Laptop/Projector
- Whiteboard
- Pencil
- Paper (Construction, Printer, and Cardstock)Pipe Cleaners
- Tape / Scissors / Markers / Crayons
- Art Supplies like stickers, washy tape, stamps, pipe cleaners, pom poms, etc.

Materials for Each Child/Group:

- Recycled materials like boxes, bottles, etc.
- Lego Pieces
- Fake Money
- Bowls
- Envelopes
- Computers, optional
- Grocery Store Items (Pretend Toys or Cut-outs)

2.1 How to Make Smart Shopping Decisions

Time Required	15 min
Group Sizes	1
Grade	K - 8
Materials Needed	
• Laptop/Projector • Whiteboard/Markers	

Learning Objectives for Module

- Understand and Apply Smart Shopping Strategies – Participants will learn how to create a budget, compare prices, and avoid impulse buying to make thoughtful financial choices.
- Develop Critical Thinking and Decision-Making Skills – Participants will analyze real-life shopping scenarios and apply the four smart shopping strategies to evaluate purchases effectively.

Ask the participants the following questions - Facilitate a discussion: "Have you ever bought something and later wished you hadn't?" "How do you decide what to buy when you go shopping?"

Shopping isn't just about buying things—it's about making good decisions with money. Being a smart shopper means knowing the difference between needs and wants, comparing prices, and sticking to a budget.

On the whiteboard, write the 4 ways to be a smart shopper and make smart shopping decisions:

1. Decide if it is a need or a want
    a. Ask: "What do you think is the difference between a need and a want?"
    b. Explain: Needs are things we must have to live (e.g., food, water, shelter, clothes). Wants are things we like to have but can live without (e.g., toys, candy, video games).

2. Make a budget
    a. Ask: "What would you do if you only had $20 to spend at the store? How would you decide what to buy?"
    b. A budget helps you plan how to spend and save money wisely. Smart shoppers plan their spending before going to the store.

3. Compare prices and find the best deals
    a. Ask: "Have you ever seen the same item at different stores for different prices?"
    b. Explain: Smart shoppers compare prices before buying. Sometimes, stores have sales, coupons, or discounts that help save money.

4. Avoid impulse buying
    a. Ask: "Have you ever seen something at the store and wanted it right away?"
    b. Explain: Impulse buying is when we buy something without thinking just because we want it. Smart shoppers wait, think, and ask themselves if they really need it.
    c. Discuss: Share tips for avoiding impulse buying:
        i. Make a shopping list and stick to it.
        ii. Wait a day before buying something expensive.
        iii. Ask: "Do I really need this?"

Let the participants know that we will be practicing these smart shopping decision tips in the classroom while learning about money.

Movie Animation / Comic / Children's Book Challenge

Once the participants know the 4 ways to be a smart shopper, have each participant pull out a certain category purchase: General shopping, Clothing, Entertainment, or Electronics / Big Ticket Stuff. General shopping refers to everything a person may buy other than the other categories like food and health and beauty supplies.

Once each participant has a category, give them the following prompt:

> Create a movie animation, comic, or children's book that follows a main character on their journey to buy a product from the category given. The movie/comic/book must show the 4 smart ways of shopping for that product as well as whether that product is a need or a want.

Below are examples of how to shop smart for each category. You may explain these ways of shopping smart before they begin making the movie animation, comic, or children's book.

> For general shopping, we would want to not shop for fun. When we shop, we wait for the sales and then shop the sales. Shop in advance for gifts. Shop elsewhere from the mall as we may be tempted to buy something we do not need.
>
> For clothing, we can shop at several different stores besides the mall. We can shop at outlet, discount, and thrift stores for cheap.
>
> For entertainment, we can go to a movie mid-day to get the cheaper price or go to a discount theater. We could also not buy popcorn or drinks as they are usually overpriced. We can look online or at the newspaper for free or low-cost events in the area.
>
> For electronics or big-ticket stuff, we can compare pricing online to other retailers. We can check the reviews of different brands and models. We can also learn the return policy for that product or company.

Participants should make a movie animation, comic, or children's book that shows a main character following these simple steps when buying from a certain category. Have participants present their movies/comics/books when everyone is finished.

Shop Smart Story Plan

Type of Project (Circle One): Movie Animation or Comic or Children's Book or Other:

____

What Objects / Characters / Media will I Use for My Story?

____

____

____

What will be the Story for My Project?

____

____

____

____

____

____

2.2 Let's Go Shopping!

Time Required	45 - 60 min
Group Sizes	1 - 3
Grade	K - 8
Materials Needed	
• Laptop/Projector • Whiteboard/Markers • Paper (Construction, Printer, and Cardstock) • Lego Pieces • Pipe Cleaners • Tape / Scissors / Markers / Crayons • Plastic Bags & Recyclables • Popsicle Sticks • Fake Money	

Learning Objective

- Understand Resource Management and Budgeting – Participants will learn how to manage a limited budget, make purchasing decisions, and balance cost and quality when acquiring raw materials to build their product.
- Apply the Engineering Design Process (EDP) – Participants will follow the steps of the Engineering Design Process (design, build, test, and improve) to create a functional product that meets specific criteria and constraints.
- Develop Collaboration and Critical Thinking Skills – Participants will work in teams to strategize, make business decisions, and problem-solve while setting up their store, purchasing materials, and constructing their product.

Let the participants know that we are going to be creating stores and products in our classroom. This will be referred to as the STEM Mall!

Place the participants into groups of 4. Each group will own a raw material.

On slips of paper, write out the following raw materials they can use to create a product later.

You can also use the following worksheet with pictures of the raw materials.

- Paper (Construction, Printer, and Cardstock)
- Lego Pieces
- Pipe Cleaners
- Tape / Scissors / Markers / Crayons
- Plastic Bags & Recyclables
- Popsicle Sticks

The following shows an example of what each material costs to buy and use:

- Lego Pieces = $1.00
- Small Cups = $3.00
- Straws = $0.50
- Pipe Cleaners = $0.50
- Bags = $4.00
- Printer Paper = $0.50

Not only will they need to buy materials, participants will need to rent equipment to make the tool with. The following shows an example of the cost of renting the equipment:

- Scissors = $1.00
- Glue = $3.00
- Tape = $1.00
- Marker = $1.00
- Crayon = $0.50

Raw Materials Slips

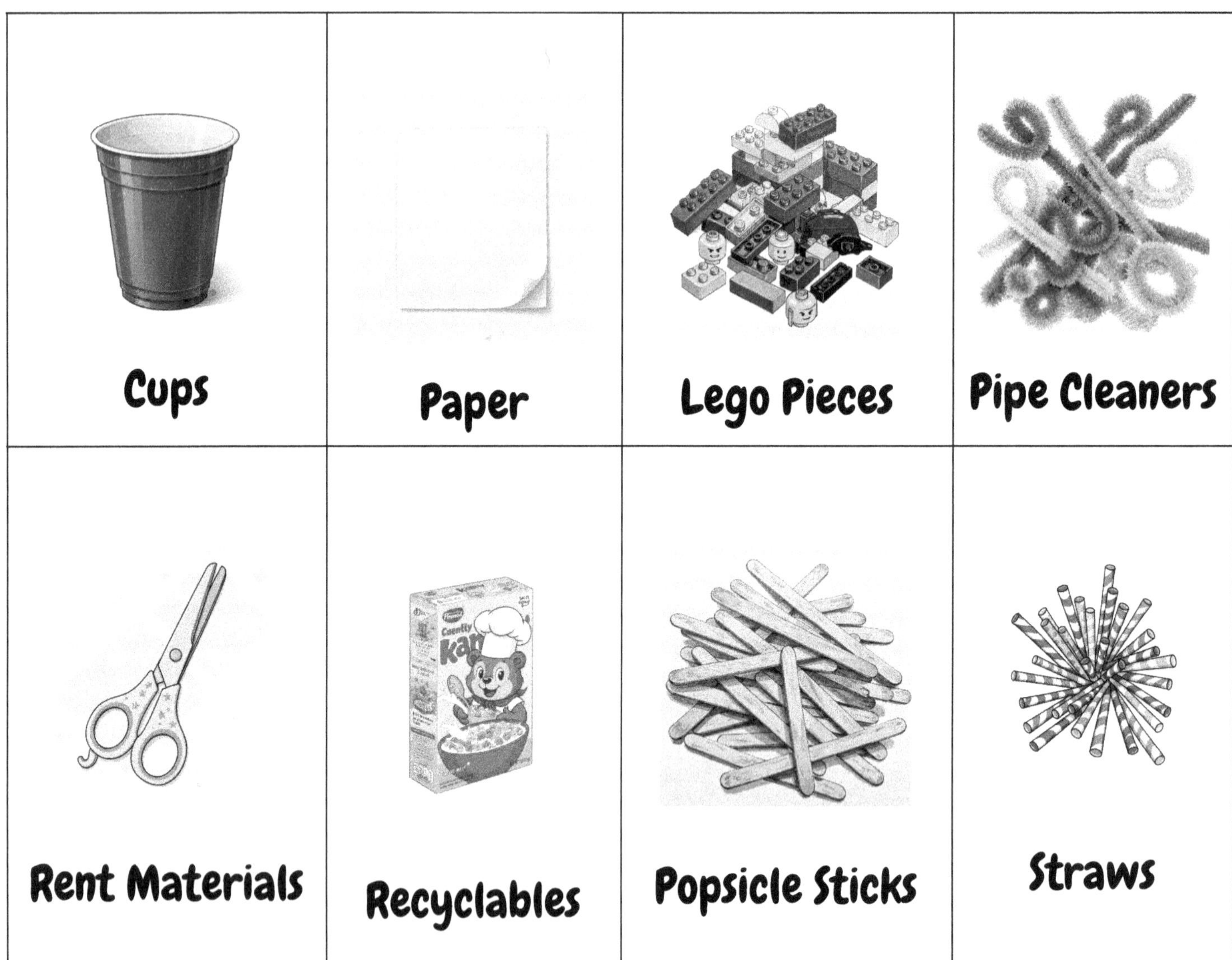

Once the groups know what raw material they will be selling, have them create a store setup with the signs and prices. This means they should have it visible what the prices are for individual and bulk buying. They should also come up with a clever name for their store. Good practice is to also have an example of what they can make with that raw material.

After the raw material stores are ready to open, have the participants get into partner groups within their raw material group. Hand each group a slip of paper that says what product they will be building to sell at their own store. See below for a list of products they can build or use worksheets to hand out products.

- Car (2 products)
- Building (2 products)
- Animal (3 products)
- Chair (4 products)
- Jewelry (8 products)
- Clothing (4 products)

Have the participants complete the worksheet below to figure out what raw materials to buy to build the product. They will need to decide on how much they will need and the cost to buy the raw materials. They will need to make a certain number of each product.

Hand each participant $50 fake dollars. It is best to use physical bills, even if they are not real. Let them know that they can look at the materials and decide which to buy based on the criteria stated in the activity. They want the tool to be stable but affordable.

Product Slips

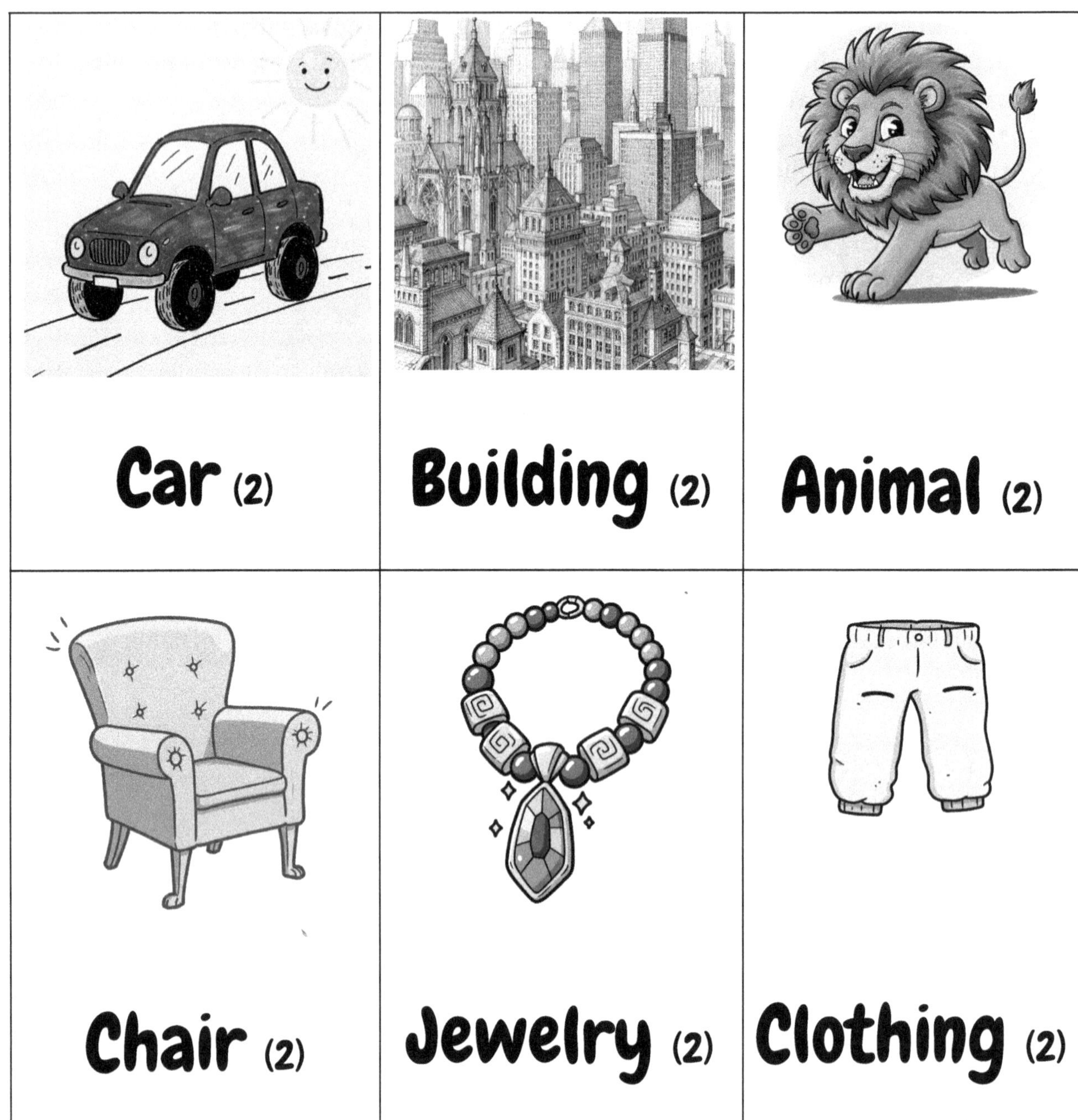

Once they know what they need to buy, have one of them from each partner group go around to each store and buy the raw materials needed to build that product. There should be two people at each raw material store that will hand their raw materials to the customer and exchange money.

Follow the EDP once the raw materials have been bought. Let the participants begin building their products.

In a partner team, use the EDP to design, build, and test the product given.

Goal: Make a product out of materials bought from each store.

Materials to be available to rent when building but will not be used as part of your design.

- Tape, scissors, Crayons / Markers

Explain when engineers work their supplies are limited, so they must plan for a small amount of supplies.

Criteria:

- The product should perform the standard actions.
- The product should not fall apart.

Constraints

- Use only the materials as specified.

Test

- Test the product based on what it should do.

My Engineering Design Process

Did it work?
YES: How can it be better?
NO: How can we fix it?

What do we have to work with and what do we want it to do?

Improve

Ask

The Goal:

What have we learned to complete this challenge?

Create

Imagine

Build it!

Plan

Draw out a few ideas on how to complete this challenge:

My Engineering Design Plan

Material	Properties	How could you use it in your design?

Draw a possible solution:

2.3 Digital Money, Bank Accounts & Online Safety

Time Required	45 - 60 min
Group Sizes	1 - 3
Grade	K - 8
Materials Needed	
• Laptop/Projector • Whiteboard/Marker • Play Money • Bowls • Envelopes • Crayons/Marker • Stickers/Stamps • Printer Paper • Computer, optional	

Learning Objective

- Understanding Money Storage: Students will learn where money is kept (e.g., piggy banks, wallets, or bank accounts) and the role of banks in protecting money.
- Practicing Bank Transactions: Students will engage in tasks like depositing, withdrawing, and transferring money to understand how bank accounts work.
- Promoting Digital Money Safety: Students will learn important rules for safely managing money online, including protecting personal information and using strong passwords.

Ask the participants: Where do people keep their money? *"In a piggy bank" "In their pockets" "In a wallet" "At the bank" "On their phone"*

People keep their money in lots of places! Some put it in a piggy bank at home. Others keep it in a wallet so they can buy things when they go out. But most grown-ups keep their money in a bank account because it's super safe there!

Ask the participants: What is a bank? *"A place where you put your money" "Where grown-ups go to get more money" "A store for money" "A place with a big safe"*

Banks keep our money safe and help us save for things we want. People can have a bank account where their money is stored.

Ask the participants: How do people get their money from a bank? *"They ask the bank people for it" "They put a card into a machine and money comes out" "They type a password and the bank lets them have money"*

They can use a debit card to spend it or take cash out of an ATM when they need it. Some people even use their phones or computers to buy things online! Instead of always using cash, people can use debit cards, credit cards, and online banking to spend their money digitally.

Be the Banker! Game

There are many ways that bank accounts and digital money can be used. Here are 5 ways we use digital money:

- **Depositing money:** People put money in the bank so they can use it later.
- **Withdrawing money:** People can take money out of their bank account using an ATM or a debit card.
- **Spending online:** People can use money in their bank account to buy things online.
- **Saving money:** Saving money in a bank account means putting your money in a safe place so it can be used when you need it, not now.
- **Earning interest (simplified for K-5):** Banks may even give a little extra money if you save it into a savings account at their bank!

Take out the picture cards and show the students different images. These images show either money stored in a bank account or physically in their hands. Participants have to decide which it is.

Put the participants into groups of 2-3 and have them decide together which option that money falls into. Give 1 minute to discuss then ask for a show of hands if the picture shows "stored in bank account" or "physically in our hands."

 Cash	 Piggy Bank
 Debit Card	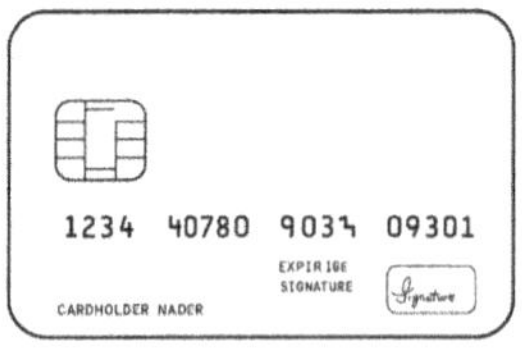 Credit Card
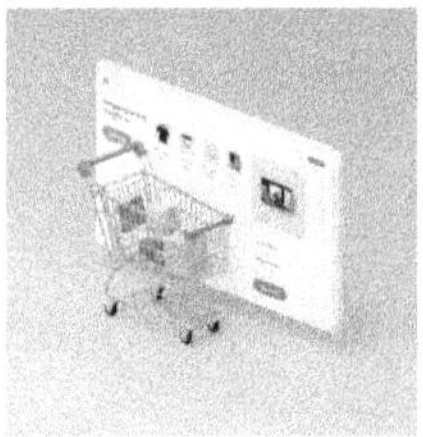 Online Shopping Cart	 ATM Machine
 Mobile Banking App	 Checks
 E-Wallet	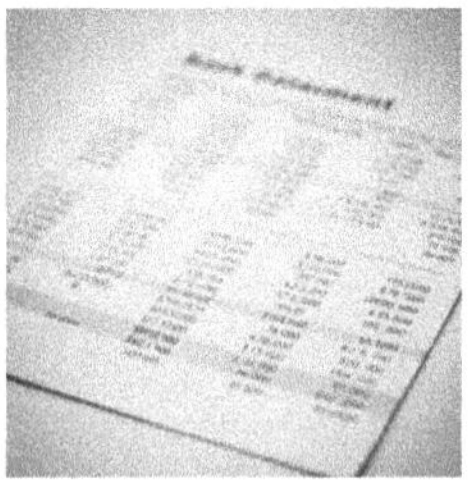 Bank Statement

Once participants have a better understanding of how bank accounts work, let them know that they are going to pretend to be bankers and customers, practicing deposits, withdrawals, and savings.

Follow the instructions below:

1. Set up the STEM Bank:
   a. Designate one area as the "STEM Bank." This is where students will go to deposit or withdraw money. Make a simple sign that says "STEM Bank" and tape it at the designated area.
   b. Choose 2 - 4 students to be "bankers" (rotate roles throughout the activity). They will take this role later.

2. Give participants their bank accounts
   a. Each student gets an envelope with a paper "bank account book" inside. This represents their bank account. They will see each bank account they have opened, type of bank account, and amount of money in each account.
   b. Point out details of each bank account - Checking may have a fee and Savings may have an interest rate that they can get back each month.

3. Have the students make an identification card for themselves.
   a. This will be used to verify that they are the bank account holder by the banker.
   b. Typically, the ID will have a picture of themselves, their name, birth date, and place they currently live in.

4. Task Slips
   a. Ask students to pick a task to complete from a bowl - This could be physical actions to be completed to earn money or a scenario in which they need to move money from one bank account to another.
   b. The task slip will have details on what needs to be done to complete the task.
   c. Once done, they will need to talk with the Bank Manager (the teacher), place their initials on the task slip, and put the task slip back in the bowl.

My Identification Card

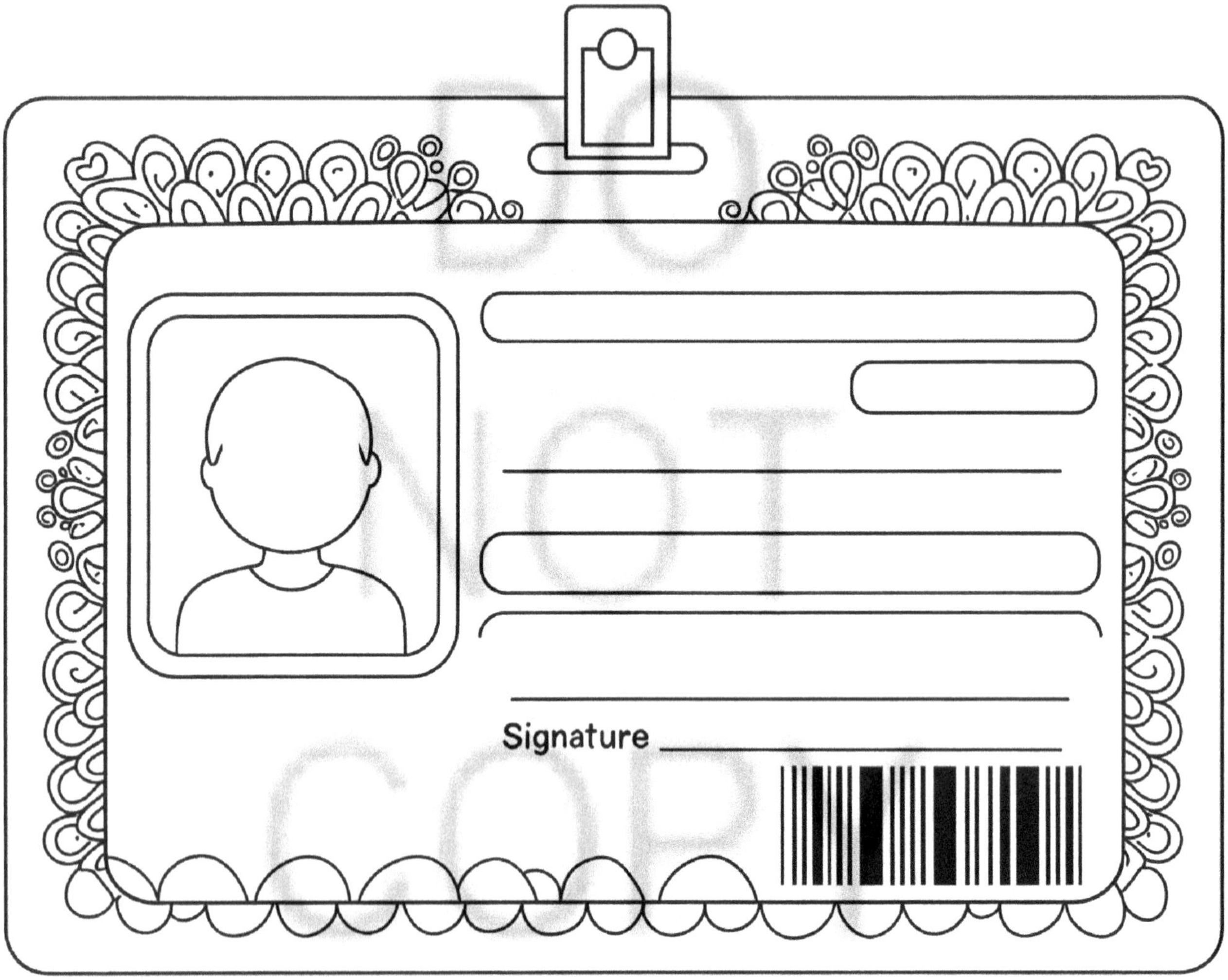

Signature

Bank Account Books: Premade

Name: ____

Bank Accounts:

- **Checking: $50**
  - Has a $5 fee for each deposit
- **Savings: $100**
  - Receive $1 for each $10 saved when complete a savings task slip

Name: ____

Bank Accounts:

- **Checking: $90**
  - Has a $10 fee for each deposit
- **Savings: $180**
  - Receive $0.50 for each $10 saved when complete a savings task slip

Name: ____

Bank Accounts:

- **Checking: $10**
  - Has a $5 fee for each deposit
- **Savings: $150**
  - Receive $2 for each $10 saved when complete a savings task slip

You are tasked to ______________________________ in the classroom. **Deposit: $20.00** Move money at the STEM Bank. Completed by: ______ ______ ______ ______ ______ ______ ______ ______
You want to buy a reward that costs $5. **Withdraw: $5.00** Go to the STEM Store to purchase a reward worth the amount. Completed by: ______ ______ ______ ______ ______ ______ ______ ______
You want to begin saving for a video game that costs $60. **Save: $30.00** Move money at the STEM Bank. Completed by: ______ ______ ______ ______ ______ ______ ______ ______
You want to give money to someone who wants lunch but does not have enough. **Withdraw: $10.00** Withdraw money at the STEM Bank. Place in the Charity bowl. Completed by: ______ ______ ______ ______ ______ ______ ______ ______
You are tasked to organize a box in the classroom. **Deposit: $15.00** Move money at the STEM Bank. Completed by: ______ ______ ______ ______ ______ ______ ______ ______
You want to begin saving for a bicycle that costs $100. **Save: $50.00** Move money at the STEM Bank. Completed by: ______ ______ ______ ______ ______ ______ ______ ______
You are tasked to sweep the floor in the classroom. Pick a spot not cleaned yet. **Deposit: $10.00** Move money at the STEM Bank. Completed by: ______ ______ ______ ______ ______ ______ ______ ______
You received a birthday gift of $25 in cash. **Deposit: $25.00** Move money at the STEM Bank. Completed by: ______ ______ ______ ______ ______ ______ ______ ______

Bank Account Slips for Banker

Name: ____

Bank Accounts:

- **Checking:** _______
  - Has a $5 fee for each deposit
- **Savings:** _______
  - Receive $1 for each $10 saved when complete a savings task slip

Name: ____

Bank Accounts:

- **Checking:** _______
  - Has a $10 fee for each deposit
- **Savings:** _______
  - Receive $0.50 for each $10 saved when complete a savings task slip

Name: ____

Bank Accounts:

- **Checking:** _______
  - Has a $5 fee for each deposit
- **Savings:** _______
  - Receive $2 for each $10 saved when complete a savings task slip

5. At the STEM Bank
    a. Get in line at the bank. Once it is their turn, they need to show the banker their ID and give their Bank Book. Once verified, the banker will hand back their ID.
    b. If they earned money, participants decide if they want to place their money into their checking or savings account. They can also split their money up if they want. They will tell the banker what they would prefer to do with their money.
        i. Make sure you remind the participants to look at the interest their savings account has to make a smart decision where their money will go.
    c. When they deposit money, the banker writes down the amount in the Bank Book for the participant and stamps or puts a sticker on it to show that the task has been completed.
    d. When they move money, the banker will add a new sheet to the participant's bank book to show where their money is currently sitting.
    e. When they make a withdrawal, the banker hands the play money to the participant and subtracts the amount from their Bank Book.
    f. In order to complete the task slip, they must show the Bank Manager (the teacher) what they accomplished and will be able to go to the Classroom Store if they choose to buy a small reward (sticker, pencil, pretend item, etc.)
        i. If it is a savings task slip, introduce "interest" and give the participant an extra $1 for every $10 they keep in their savings account.
6. Do more task slips
    a. Pick another task to complete.

After all the task slips are completed, have the participants sit in front of the whiteboard with their Bank Books in their hands. Ask the following questions to reflect on the STEM Bank simulation.

Depositing Money:

- How did it feel when you deposited your money into your account?
- Why is it important to put some of your money into savings instead of spending it all?
- What is the difference between depositing money and spending it?

Withdrawing Money:

- What did you need to think about before deciding to withdraw money?
- How did you feel when you had to choose how much money to take out?
- How does withdrawing money affect how much you have in your account?

Saving Money:

- Why is saving money important for the future?
- How can saving money help you reach your goals (e.g., buying something you want)?
- How did saving money in the simulation help you feel more prepared for future needs?

Understanding Money Management:

- What did you learn about managing money from this activity?
- What are some ways you can make sure you don't spend all your money right away?
- How do you decide what to save and what to spend?

Making Choices:

- How did you decide how much to save and how much to spend or withdraw?
- What was the most challenging part of the simulation?
- If you could do the simulation again, what would you do differently?

Protecting Digital Money - Online Safety

Because we view and use our money online through bank accounts and online shopping, we need to be safe with our personal information like passwords, names, date of births, social security numbers, etc. that could be used by others we do not know.

Here are some key safety rules to have when using digital money methods:

- **Ask a Trusted Adult** – Always ask an adult before using digital money.
- **Keep Personal Information Private** – Never share bank details, passwords, or card numbers.
- **Keep passwords secret** – Never share your passwords or PINs with anyone except a trusted adult.
- **Use strong passwords** – Create passwords with a mix of letters, numbers, and symbols to make them hard to guess.
- **Be careful with links** – Don't click on links in emails or messages that seem suspicious or ask for personal information.
- **Only use safe websites** – Look for a padlock symbol and "https://" in the web address before entering any information.
- **Watch out for scams** – Some people online may try to trick you into giving them money. If something seems too good to be true, like free money or prizes, it's probably a trick!
- **Log out when done** – If you use a shared device, always log out of accounts when finished.
- **Check with an adult** – If you ever feel unsure about something online, ask a trusted adult for help.

Create a public service announcement that goes over these key safety rules others should follow when using digital money methods. It could be a poster, children's book, pamphlet, animation, etc. Think outside the box.

2.4 Grocery Store Role Play with Digital Payments

Time Required	45 - 60 min
Group Sizes	1
Grade	K - 5
Materials Needed	
• Whiteboard/Marker • Laptop/Projector • Crayons/Markers • Play Money • Grocery Store Items (Pretend Toys or Cut-outs)	

Learning Objective

- Participants will identify and explain how to use debit cards, credit cards, and checks to make purchases.
- Participants will demonstrate an understanding of responsible money management and payment methods in a simulated grocery store scenario.
- Participants will practice critical thinking and decision-making about when to use each payment method.

Begin by asking the participants what they know about paying for items in a store. How do people typically pay for groceries? *Debit cards, credit cards, checks, etc.*

Ask the participants: What is the difference between a debit card, credit card, and check?

- **Debit Cards:** Money is taken directly from a bank account to pay for items.
- **Credit Cards:** Money is borrowed, and the person needs to pay it back later (explaining briefly that it's like borrowing money).
- **Checks:** A written order to a bank to pay money from a person's bank account to another party.

Read the following to the participants to explain each way you can purchase items from a store.

Debit Cards:

"Let's talk about debit cards first. A debit card is a card that is connected directly to your bank account. When you use it to buy something, the money comes out of your account right away. It's like using your own money."

Example: "Imagine you have $20 in your bank account, and you go to buy a toy that costs $15. When you use your debit card, $15 will be taken out of your bank account and you'll have $5 left."

"If you don't have enough money in your bank account, you can't use the debit card to buy things. You can only spend the money you have in the bank."

"Do you think it's important to know how much money is in your bank account before using a debit card? Why?"

Credit Cards:

"Now, let's talk about credit cards. A credit card is different because it's like borrowing money from a bank or a company. When you use a credit card, you don't take money from your own bank account right away. Instead, you're borrowing the money and you need to pay it back later."

Example: "Imagine you buy a toy that costs $20 with a credit card. You don't pay the store right away, but the company who gave you the credit card will pay the store for you. Then, you have to pay back that $20 to the company later. Sometimes, if you don't pay it back right away, you might owe extra money called interest."

"Credit cards can be helpful if you need to buy something but don't have the money right now. But remember, you always have to pay the money back or else you might owe more."

"Why do you think people need to be careful when using a credit card?"

Checks:

"Finally, let's talk about checks. A check is a piece of paper you can write on to tell your bank to pay someone else money from your bank account."

Example: "Let's say you want to pay someone for a toy, but you don't have cash with you. You can write a check for $10, and the bank will take $10 from your bank account and give it to the person you are paying."

"Unlike debit cards, you can't just swipe a check or use it like a card. You have to write it out and give it to the person or business, and then they take it to their bank to cash it."

"When might someone want to use a check instead of a card or cash? Do you think writing a check is easy or hard?"

Comparing debit cards, credit cards, and checks:

"Now that we've learned about all three, let's compare them. I'm going to ask you some questions, and I want you to think about which payment method would work best in each situation."

- "If you want to spend money you already have in your bank account, which payment method would you use? (Answer: Debit card)"
- "If you don't have enough money in your bank account but need to buy something right away, which payment method might you use? (Answer: Credit card)"
- "If you want to pay someone you owe money to but don't have cash, which payment method could you use? (Answer: Check)"

"What are the key differences between these three payment methods? What do you think is the most important thing to remember when using them?"

Follow the steps below to have a grocery store simulation with digital payments:

1. Have each participant create their own debit card and credit card. Hand 1 blank check template each to the participants.
   a. Give each participant a set amount that they have on each of their cards and bank account for their check. Have them write it down somewhere for future reference.

2. Setting up the grocery store
   a. Assign Roles: Divide students into groups of 2-3, where each group will take turns being the Customer and Cashier.
      i. Customer Roles: Students will use play money or a check, debit card, or credit card to make purchases at the grocery store.
      ii. Cashier Roles: Students will calculate totals for the customers and process the payment.
   b. Set up a "grocery store" in the classroom with grocery items and price tags. You may use small toys that look like grocery items or cut-outs. See templates below.

My Debit Card, Credit Card, and Checks

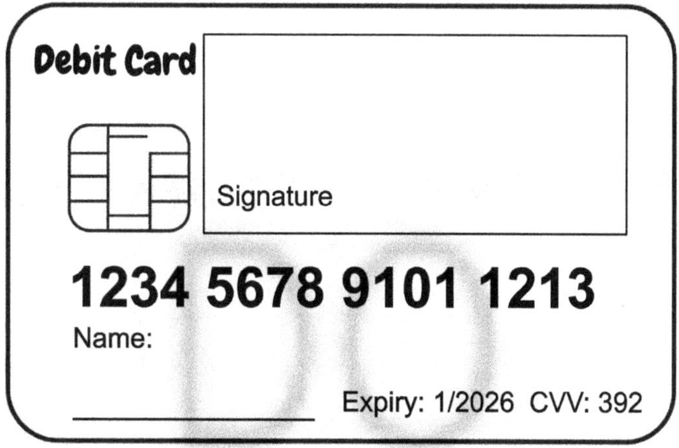

Credit Card

Signature

1415 1617 1819 2021

Name:

_______________ Expiry: 5/2026 CVV: 105

PERSONAL CHECK

Date _______________

Payee _______________________________ [ ]

Amount _______________________________

Memo _______________ Signature _______________

BANK

Grocery Store Items Cards

 Apple = $1.00 each	 Loaf of Bread = $2.50
 Milk = $3.00	 Cereal (Box) = $3.50
 Bag of Chips = $4.00	 Chicken Breast (Per Pound) = $4.00
 Peanut Butter (Jar) = $2.25	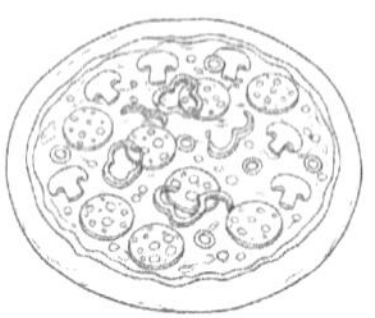 Frozen Pizza = $7.00
 Ice Cream (1 Pint) = $4.00	 Yogurt (Cup) = $1.25

Price Tag Templates

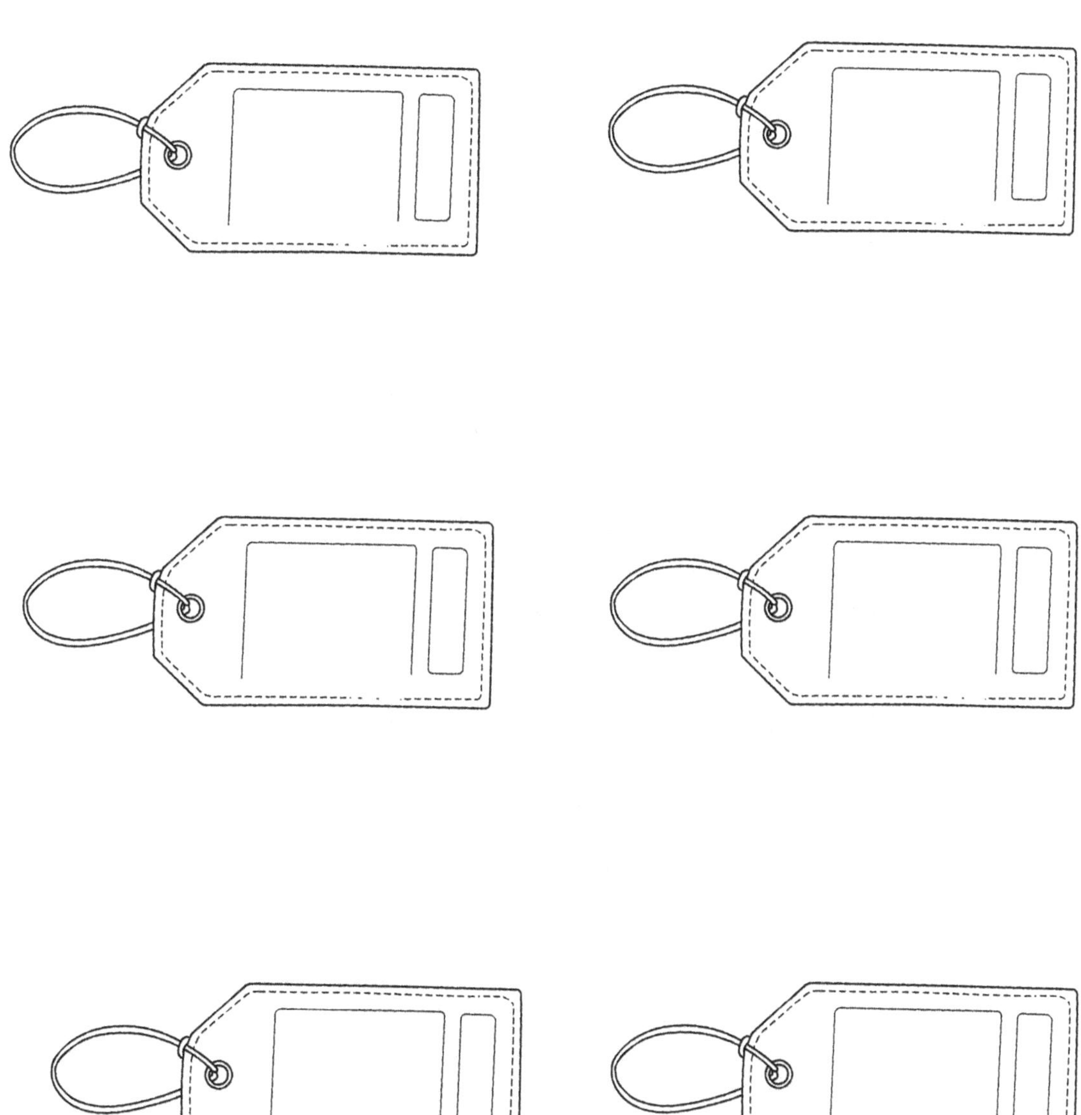

Receipt Templates

3. Shopping
    a. Allow the Customers to "shop" by picking 3-5 items from the store (or choosing from grocery item images). Each item has a price tag.
        i. Example Scenario: A bottle of juice ($3), a loaf of bread ($2), and a bag of apples ($4).

4. Checkout
    a. The customer goes to the "Cashier" with their items and checks out their items. The cashier tallies the amount due.
    b. Extension: Calculate sales tax
        i. The cashier will calculate 6% of the total cost before tax.
        ii. Sales Tax Calculation: $5.75 x 6% = $0.35
        iii. Total with Tax: $5.75 + $0.35 = $6.10
    c. The customer chooses one of the following payment methods by pulling a slip out of a bowl. Follow the steps based on the slip they pull out:
        i. Debit Card: The cashier will simulate swiping the debit card and subtract the amount from the customer's total balance.
        ii. Credit Card: The cashier will simulate processing the credit card payment, but explain that the customer will need to pay back the money later.
        iii. Check: The customer fills out a check (play check) to pay for the total. The cashier will stamp or mark it as "paid."

5. Role Switch
    a. After the transaction, students will switch roles, so everyone gets a chance to be both a customer and a cashier.

After the role play, ask the students to reflect on their decisions and how using different payment methods impacts money management. Gather the participants to the whiteboard and discuss:

- How did it feel to use a debit card, credit card, or check to pay for items?
- What was different about using a debit card versus a credit card?
- Why is it important to know how much money you have before using a debit card or credit card?
- Why might someone choose to pay with a check instead of a debit card?

Summarize the importance of understanding different payment methods, how to use them responsibly, and the importance of budgeting money.

2.5 Smart Shoppers Challenge

Time Required	30 min
Group Sizes	1 - 3
Grade	3 - 5
Materials Needed	
• Whiteboard/Marker • Laptop/Projector	

Learning Objective

- Participants will compare prices of similar items, calculating the price per unit (e.g., per ounce, per item).
- Participants will make informed decisions based on value, not just total price.
- Participants will apply their understanding of price comparison to everyday shopping situations.

Begin by asking the participants: Have you ever had to choose between two similar products at the store? How did you decide which one to buy? Do you always choose the cheaper option?

Let them know that today they are going to practice being Smart Shoppers. We're going to compare prices and make decisions based on the best deal.

Sometimes, two different brands or types of the same item cost different amounts. The lower price does not always mean it's the best deal. We have to think about how much we get for the price.

Using your computer, show two different brands of cereal on a local grocery store website. Make sure the costs and sizes are different. We'll use the following example:

> Brand A - $3.50 for 12 ounces
> Brand B - $4.00 for 15 ounces

Ask the following questions about the cereal: Which box is cheaper? Is the price tag the only thing that matters when making a decision?

If we look at how much we are getting, we can figure out which one gives us more cereal for less money. Let's calculate together.

Brand A - $3.50 / 12 ounces = $0.29 per ounce
Brand B - $4.00 / 15 ounces = $0.27 per ounce

Brand B gives a better deal because it costs less per ounce even though the total price is higher.

Divide the class into small groups of 2-3 participants. Give each group 2-3 pairs of items to compare (e.g. two types of juice, two different brands of shoes, etc.) Make sure the pairs have different brands or types with differing prices. Hand out the worksheet to record the pricing comparisons.

In the groups, participants should write down the price of each item and calculate the price per unit (e.g. price per ounce, price per item). At the end, they should decide which item gives the best deal. On the whiteboard, write out the items that are being compared and have the participants write which their group thinks is the best deal. Walk around to assist with calculations or guide discussions on comparing items.

Bring the class together and discuss the answers on the whiteboard. Do the math together or have participants write their math on the whiteboard. Ask the following reflection questions: How did the size or quantity of the item affect the price comparison? What made the best deal - the lowest price or the amount you get for the price? How could you apply this skill next time you go shopping?

Now that we know how to compare prices, we can be Smart Shoppers and make better decisions about where to spend our money.

Smart Shopper Math Challenge

Juice Bottles

Bottle A: $2.99 for 64 ounces

Bottle B: $3.50 for 80 ounces

Which bottle gives you more juice for your money? (circle)

Cheese Blocks

Brand X: $5.00 for 16 ounces

Brand Y: $4.50 for 14 ounces

Which cheese is the better deal per ounce? (circle)

Snack Packs

10-pack of crackers: $6.00

12-pack of crackers: $7.00

Which pack gives you a lower cost per cracker pack? (circle)

Milk Cartons

Small carton (half-gallon): $2.50

Large carton (full gallon): $4.00

Which option saves you money per gallon? (circle)

Sneakers

Brand A: $45.00, lasts about 6 months

Brand B: $60.00, lasts about 1 year

Which brand is the better value over time? (circle)

T-Shirts

Store A: $10 each or 3 for $25

Store B: $8 each but no discount on multiples

Which store offers the better deal if you want 3 shirts? (circle)

Laundry Detergent

Brand A: $12.00 for 100 loads

Brand B: $8.50 for 70 loads

Which detergent has the lower cost per load? (circle)

Toilet Paper

6-pack: $5.99

12-pack: $10.50

Which option gives you a lower price per roll? (circle)

Smart Shopper Math Challenge

Paper Towels

Pack of 4: $4.50

Pack of 8: $8.00

Which pack is the better deal per roll? (circle)

Headphones

Brand A: $30.00, with a 1-year warranty

Brand B: $40.00, with a 2-year warranty

Which is the better investment based on longevity? (circle)

Notebook Paper

Store A: 200 sheets for $3.50

Store B: 250 sheets for $4.00

Which store offers the better price per sheet? (circle)

Buying in Bulk vs. Single Purchase

Single bottle of shampoo: $4.50

Pack of 3 bottles: $12.00

Is the bulk purchase a better deal? (circle)

Discounted Items

A backpack costs $40 but is on sale for 25% off

A similar backpack is $32 with no discount

Which is the better deal after applying the discount? (circle)

Restaurant Meal vs. Cooking at Home

Fast food meal: $9 per person

Cooking at home: $20 for 4 people

Which option saves more money per meal? (circle)

2.6 The Super Saver Coupon Challenge

Time Required	30 min
Group Sizes	1 - 3
Grade	3 - 5
Materials Needed	
• Whiteboard/Marker • Laptop/Projector	

Learning Objective

- Participants will learn how to use coupons to save money while shopping and practice basic math skills related to discounts.
- Help participants understand what coupons are, how they work, and why people use them.

Ask the participants if they have ever seen their parents or someone they know use a coupon at a store. What do they think a coupon does? Encourage them to share their experiences. What sort of coupons are out there? Some may mention grocery store coupons, online discounts, or deals on toys or clothes.

Explain that coupons are like special tickets that help you save money when you buy something. Instead of paying full price, a coupon gives you a discount. Write some examples of coupons on the whiteboard. Some examples of a coupon are:

> "$1.00 Off Any Cereal"
> "Save 20% on Your Next Purchase"
> "Buy One Get One Free on Juice" (BOGO)

Ask them what they notice about these coupons and which coupon do they think saves the most money. It really depends on what is being purchased!

There are many reasons people use coupons.

- Saving Money - Instead of paying full price, you keep extra money in your pocket!
- Smart Shopping - Some people use coupons to buy things they already need at a lower cost. Some may buy things that they consider a luxury for much cheaper!
- More for Less - The BOGO deals mean you get extra items without paying more.

How do you think stores benefit from giving out coupons? Stores give out coupons because they want more people to come and shop. When you see a coupon for something you like, you might go to that store to buy it. While you are there, you might buy other things, making it worth it for the store. Even though the store gives you a discount, they still make money because more people are shopping with them. This is called a win-win. You save money, the store gets more customers!

There are typically 3 types of coupons:

- Dollar-off Coupons: Takes money off the total price like "$2 off a loaf of bread" or "$15 off a $50 purchase."
- Percentage-Off Coupons: Gives a discount by percentage like "20% off your purchase" or "10% off all shoes."
- Buy One, Get One Free (BOGO): You buy one item and get another for free. There will be many variations of this coupon like "Buy 2 Get 3 Free" or "Buy 1 Get 50% Off 2nd."

Give the participants different coupons and a set of price tags for grocery items. Ask them to match the correct coupon to the right item (e.g. a coupon for $0.50 off milk should go with a milk price tag.) Have the participants calculate the new price after applying the coupon. Complete the worksheet to practice this.

Once done practicing, you can set up the grocery store simulation again and provide a few coupons. Have them conduct the same steps but apply coupons and calculate how much they save using coupons.

During reflection, ask: How did using coupons help you save money? Was it better to use a percentage-off coupon or a dollar-off coupon? Why? What are some ways your family could use coupons when shopping?

The Super Saver Coupon Challenge

Part 1: Match the Coupon to the Item

Draw a line to connect each coupon to the correct item.

$1.00 Off Any Box of Cereal	Apples ($1.00 Each)
Buy One Get One Free on Apples	Cereal ($4.00 Per Box)
Save 20% on Any Toy	Toy ($10.00)
$0.50 Off Any Loaf of Bread	Bread ($3.00)

Part 2: Calculate the Discount

Use the coupon to find the final price of each item.

- Milk - $5.00 (Save $2.00) → New Price: ______________
- Pizza - $8.00 (25% Off) → New Price: ______________
- Movie Ticket - $12.00 ($3.00 Off) → New Price: ______________

Part 3: Smart Shopping Questions

- If you had a coupon for "Buy One Get One Free on Juice" and you only need one, would you still use the coupon? Why or why not?

  ____

  ____

  ____

- Which coupon do you think saves the most money? A "$5.00 Off" coupon or a "10% Off" coupon on a $50 item?

  ____

- If your total bill is $20.00 and you have a coupon for "Save $5.00", how much will you pay?

  ____

2.7 Recap

Time Required	15 - 20 min
Group Sizes	1
Grade	K - 8
Materials Needed	
• Paper • Pencil • Whiteboard	

Learning Objective

- Recall and apply terms and ideas related to finance, money, and engineering through an interactive activity.
- Provide an informal opportunity to evaluate participants' comprehension of key topics covered in class.
- Develop the ability to convey and recognize ideas through drawing and verbal explanation.
- Build teamwork and camaraderie by encouraging participants to work together during the game.

On the whiteboard, write **"One thing that I learned today ..."**

Have each participant write a complete statement. Be mindful of space on the whiteboard as we want all participants' writing to make it on the whiteboard.

Take a picture of this and send in the daily summary to parents.

After everyone has written on the whiteboard, discuss as a group. If some key learning points did not get reinforced through the activity, remind the participants of those activities that were done during the day and what they learned from it.

This is a great activity to get participants up and about and reinforce the key learning for them. It is best suited for an end of day recap.

Module 3: Money Doesn't Grow on Trees

In this module, participants will explore various career options and gain financial literacy by learning about job responsibilities, salaries, and work environments. They will understand entrepreneurship, business planning, and sales tax, as well as practice money management, decision-making, and customer engagement in a STEM Market setting, reinforcing their financial responsibility and entrepreneurial skills.

Materials

Materials for the Class

- Teacher Laptop / Projector
- Poster Boards (1 per group)
- Markers / Crayons
- Pencil
- Tape / Scissors / Markers / Crayons
- Paper (Construction, Printer, and Cardstock)
- Tape / Scissors / Markers / Crayons
- Art Supplies like stickers, washy tape, stamps, pipe cleaners, pom poms, etc.
- Play Money
- Envelopes
- Recycled materials like boxes, bottles, etc.

Materials for Each Child/Group

- Computer/Device
- Stuffed Animal
- Bowls
- Doll Bed & Small Blanket
- Small Clothes in Basket
- Plastic Dishes
- Sponge
- Trash Bin
- Recycle Bin
- Clean Trash & Plastic Bottles
- Small Broom/Dust Pan
- Small Cloths
- Bin of Small Toys
- Small Plant with Water Dropper
- Lego Pieces

3.1 Time to Find a Job

Time Required	30 min
Group Sizes	1
Grade	K - 8
Materials Needed	
• Laptop/Projector • Whiteboard/Markers • Computer / Device	

Learning Objectives for Module

- Explore Career Options and Financial Literacy – Participants will research and analyze various careers, understanding job responsibilities, salaries, work hours, and job satisfaction to make informed career choices in the future.

- Apply Creative and Digital Storytelling Skills – Participants will use storytelling techniques and digital tools (such as animations or presentations) to illustrate a day in the life of their chosen career, demonstrating understanding in an engaging format.
- Develop Research and Presentation Skills – Participants will gather information about a profession, organize their findings, and effectively communicate their career insights through a visual or animated presentation to their peers.

Ask the participants what they want to be when they grow up. Write responses on the white board. Explain that, for us to earn money, we need to have a job of some sort. This could mean that we work for a company, sell products in our own business, or provide services to the community. Either way, we will need to earn money through giving back to the community.

Explain to the participants that we are going to research the job that they want to have when they are older. We will learn how much money they would make, what they would do, how many hours they may work, and what satisfactions they would get from that job. We must keep these in mind whenever we accept a job to earn money.

Have the participants decide on the job they want to research more about. Complete the worksheet below when researching the specific job.

Career Research

What do people in this career do?

____

____

____

What types of problems do they solve?

____

____

____

What are some examples of technologies or solutions created by people in this career?

____

____

____

How much money can you make in this line of work? ____________________

What kind of education do you need to get into this career?

____

What are the skills required to be successful in this career?

____

____

____

What are some good colleges / universities to pursue this education?

____

____

____

Once finished researching their dream job, have the participants complete the following prompt to create a movie animation/story presentation about that job:

> **A Day in the Life of… :** Create a movie animation/story presentation that follows the day in the life of your dream job. Have the main character show what you would be doing at that job as well as how you would be paid doing that job.

Note to Coach: You may use Programming II – Alice curriculum to create the movie animations. Follow the curriculum to understand how to design, build, and program animations in Alice. Or simply use PowerPoint or Google Slides to create a story presentation.

Pass out paper and pencils/markers to the participants. Have them come up with a plan for their story. Have them write down what they want their story to accomplish, what kind of objects/media they want to include, what types of programming blocks they may need if applicable, and what they want the background/appearance to look like. (Note: have them draw out their background and characters)

After they have come up with a plan, have them show it to you and decide whether they need more detail or not. After their plans have been finalized, allow them to begin working on their movies/presentations.

At the end of each day, campers should save their program/presentation to their computers or share the project with you with a link. To do so, have them select file->save world as. Tell them to remember where they saved their file so they can find it again later.

Once done creating the movie animation/story presentation, have the participants present their career to the classroom. Have other participants ask questions to the presenter about their career of choice. Provide a congratulations sticker for presenting their project.

Your Career Story Plan

Type of Project (Circle One): Movie Animation or Story Presentation or Other:

What Objects / Characters / Media will I Use for My Story?

What will be the Story for My Project?

3.2 Allowances

Time Required	45 - 60 min
Group Sizes	1 - 3
Grade	K - 5
Materials Needed	
• Laptop/Projector • Whiteboard/Markers • Stuffed Animal • Bowls • Pom Poms • Doll Bed & Small Blanket • Small Clothes in Basket • Plastic Dishes • Sponge • Trash Bin • Recycle Bin • Clean Trash & Plastic Bottles • Small Broom/Dust Pan • Small Cloths • Bin of Small Toys • Small Plant with Water Dropper • Envelopes • Play Money	

Learning Objective

- Understand the Concept of Allowance: Participants will learn what an allowance is, why some children receive it, and how it can help teach money management skills.
- Practice Earning and Managing Money: Through hands-on activities, participants will complete chores to earn pretend money, make decisions about saving or spending, and experience the value of financial responsibility.
- Develop Decision-Making and Budgeting Skills: Participants will reflect on their earnings, consider the importance of saving for larger goals, and practice making thoughtful financial choices.

Start by letting the participants know that we are going to be learning about allowances today. This may be something they receive at home. Have you ever heard of an allowance before? Do you receive one? If you don't, that's fine! Everything we learn today can be applied any time you receive a small amount of money for certain events like your birthday.

An allowance is money that some kids get from their parents or guardians. You might earn it by helping out at home or it could be given to you to help you learn how to manage your money. Why do you think some parents might give their kids an allowance? *To buy things, to save money for bigger items, to learn about money, as a reward for chores, etc.*

Allowances can help kids learn how to make good choices with money. Some allowances are given per chore while other allowances are a set amount of money per week no matter the chore completed. Imagine you get $5 a week - What would you do with it? On the whiteboard, write out the responses and ask if it falls under Spend, Save, or Donate.

There are different things we can do with our money. We can spend it on things we want now, save it for something bigger later, or even donate it to help others. Why do you think it's important to save some of your money instead of spending it all at once? Encourage discussion about saving bigger goals, being prepared for emergencies/surprises, and making thoughtful decisions.

What if you really wanted a new toy that costs $10, but you only have $5? What could you do? Have the participants think through solutions - Saving more money, doing extra chores, waiting instead of spending right away, etc.

Allowances help us learn how to manage money wisely. Let's practice making smart money choices with a game of allowances.

Game of Allowances

1. Together as a class, ask the participants for chores they are asked to do at home. Write on the whiteboard for our "Classroom Pretend Chore Chart." Below are a few examples you can have on the chart for the classroom. We are going to pretend that we get paid per chore but know that most of the time allowances are given as a set amount like $10 per week for any amount of chores that need to be completed.

    - Set a monetary amount for each chore - You can discuss with the group what seems like a reasonable amount to receive for that chore.

        i. Some chores are set lower than other chores since they happen all the time. Some chores are set higher than other chores since they happen at random intervals like deep cleaning your room or vacuuming a room.

1. Setting the Table for Dinner = $0.50
2. Feeding a Pet = $1.00
3. Make Your Bed (Once a Day) = $0.50
4. Put Toys Away (Once a Day) = $0.50
5. Clear the Table for Dinner = $0.50
6. Sweep the Floor = $2.00
7. Vacuum a Room = $2.50
8. Water the Plants = $2.00
9. Help with Laundry = $3.00
10. Take Out the Trash = $2.00
11. Clean Your Bedroom = $5.00
12. Wash the Dishes = $2.50
13. Organize Books / Toys = $5.00
14. Rake Leaves = $5.00
15. Read to a Younger Sibling = $2.00
16. Help a Sibling with Homework = $3.00

2. In the classroom, set up certain chore stations that the participants can complete to receive an allowance.

- Pet Care Station
  - i. Setup: A table with a stuffed animal and a bowl.
  - ii. Task: Students "feed" their pet by placing pretend food (beans, paper cutouts, or pom-poms) in the bowl.
  - iii. Earnings: $1.00

- Bed-Making Station
  - i. Setup: A small cot, doll bed, or blanket on a table.
  - ii. Task: Students neatly spread the blanket and fluff a pillow.
  - iii. Earnings: $1.50

- Laundry Folding Station
  - i. Setup: A basket with small towels, socks, or doll clothes.
  - ii. Task: Students fold laundry neatly and stack it.
  - iii. Earnings: $2.00

- Dishwashing Station
  - i. Setup: Plastic plates, cups, and a sponge.
  - ii. Task: Students pretend to wash and dry dishes, then stack them.
  - iii. Earnings: $1.50

- Table-Setting Station
    1. Setup: A table with plates, cups, napkins, and utensils.
    2. Task: Students properly set the table for a meal.
    3. Earnings: $1.00

- Trash & Recycling Station
    1. Setup: A mini trash bin with crumpled paper and a recycling bin with plastic bottles.
    2. Task: Students sort and throw away trash correctly.
    3. Earnings: $1.50

- Sweeping & Cleaning Station
    1. Setup: A small broom and dustpan or a microfiber cloth for wiping a table.
    2. Task: Students sweep a small area or wipe down a surface.
    3. Earnings: $2.00

- Toy Organization/Cleaning Station
    1. Setup: A bin of scattered small toys, books, or blocks. Wipes/Cloth
    2. Task: Students put items back in their correct place.
    3. Earnings: $1.00

- Plant Watering Station
    1. Setup: A small potted plant and a water dropper or small watering can.
    2. Task: Students water the plant without overflooding it.
    3. Earnings: $1.50

- Helping Hand Station
    1. Setup: A whiteboard with a "kindness" task (e.g., help a classmate, push in chairs).
    2. Task: Students complete a good deed for a classmate.
    3. Earnings: $1.00

3. Hand out an envelope to each participant to hold their earnings - They can decorate the envelope to be their "wallet." Have the participants go to an open chore station and complete that chore.

4. When a participant finishes a chore, they should raise their hand to be checked by the teacher. You can give them the earnings if you deem the chore completed.

5. They can use this allowance to go to the Classroom Store to get some rewards like stickers, small toys, etc or place into their bank accounts that they had from Module 2 Activity 3.

Once done, ask the participants the following reflection questions - You can also use the worksheet:

- How did it feel to earn money for completing chores?
- Were some chores harder than others? Why?
- Do you think it's fair to earn different amounts of money for different chores?
- Why do people have to do chores even if they don't get paid for them?

- What did you do with the money you earned? Did you save it or spend it?
- How did you decide whether to save or spend your money?
- If you had a chance to do the simulation again, would you make different choices with your money?

- Which chore did you enjoy the most? Why?
- Which chore was the most challenging? What made it hard?
- Do you think real-life chores take the same amount of effort as the ones in the game?

- Do you think kids should get an allowance for doing chores? Why or why not?
- How do you think families decide what chores should be done at home?
- What would you do if you wanted to buy something but didn't have enough money?
- How can doing chores help prepare you for responsibilities when you grow up?

Allowance Reflection 

How did it feel to earn money for completing chores? Were some chores harder than others? How about chores that were easier? Why?

Do you think it's fair to earn different amounts of money for different chores?

If you had a chance to do the Chore Game again, would you make different choices with your money? Why or why not?

Do you think real-life chores take the same amount of effort as the ones in the Chores Game? Why or why not?

Do you think kids should get an allowance for doing chores? Why or why not?

How can doing chores help prepare you for responsibilities when you grow up?

3.3 Making a Product

Time Required	45 - 60 min
Group Sizes	1 class
Grade	K - 8
Materials Needed	
• Laptop/Projector • Whiteboard/Markers • Paper (Construction, Printer, and Cardstock) • Lego Pieces • Pipe Cleaners • Tape / Scissors / Markers / Crayons • Plastic Bags & Recyclables • Popsicle Sticks • Fake Money	

Learning Objective

- Understand Entrepreneurship and Business Planning – Participants will learn what it means to be an entrepreneur, how businesses are created, and the key steps involved in developing a business plan, including naming their business, designing a logo, and selecting products to sell.
- Apply Financial Literacy and Cost Management – Participants will practice budgeting, making purchasing decisions, and calculating costs by managing their business grant money, determining the cost of materials, and understanding the concept of Cost of Goods Sold (COGS).
- Develop Critical Thinking and Problem-Solving Skills – Participants will strategize how to create stable and affordable products using limited resources, adjusting their business plans as needed while considering product quality, cost, and market demand.

Ask the participants if they know someone who owns a business. Maybe a relative in their family or a family friend. Explain that this person is who we would call an entrepreneur.

An entrepreneur turns an idea into a company to make money. Entrepreneurs can come from all over the world. They are diverse and can even be children! All entrepreneurs need are great ideas, put the idea to action, and the ability to dedicate to the idea.

Let's learn how to make a business and sell products to make money!

Explain that we will be creating a business to sell products that the students will be building and improving. They will be able to "purchase" materials to be able to make the products for their business. Then, we will have a STEM Market at the end where customers can go to each store and "purchase" the products the businesses made.

First, we need to decide what business and products we are going to be selling. Have the students decide if they want to be the sole business owner or have a business partner. Once that is decided, hand out the "My Business" worksheet. Students will need to fill out the worksheet with their business name, slogan, logo, list of products, etc. Most important information on this worksheet for now is the business name and list of products.

Hand out the "Product Ideas You Could Make" document to give students some ideas of what products they could make. Make sure they understand that they can go outside of these ideas and make their own products.

Note to Coach: You will keep the "My Business" worksheets for future classes so you know what the business plan was and if they need to make any updates.

My Business

Name of Business ____

Slogan ____

Logo:

What are you selling for your business? Why?

____

____

____

____

____

____

Product Ideas You Could Make

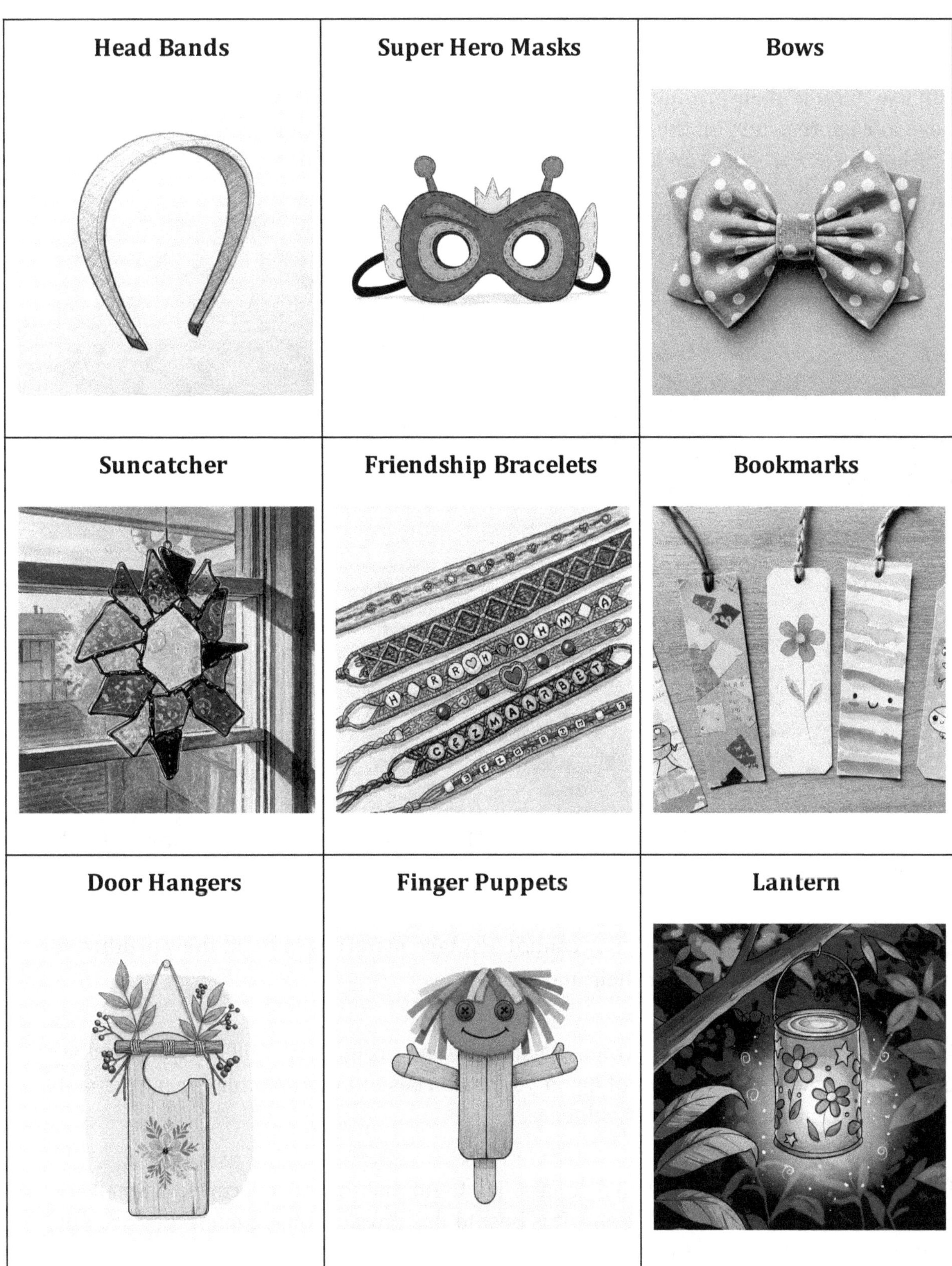
Head Bands
Super Hero Masks
Bows
Suncatcher
Friendship Bracelets
Bookmarks
Door Hangers
Finger Puppets
Lantern

Note to Coach: Before or while the businesses are filling out the worksheet, you need to have the "STEM Store" ready in the room. It is a section where all the materials students can use to build their products are displayed alongside price signs. You will also need to have a "cash register" on the table for when the STEM Store opens. See examples below of what the STEM Store can look like and pricing you can provide.

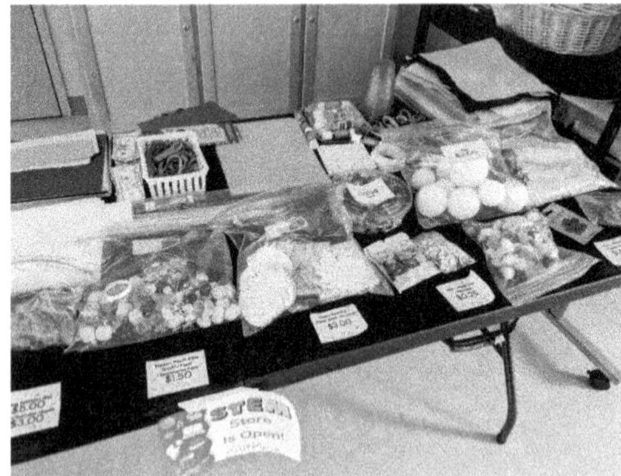

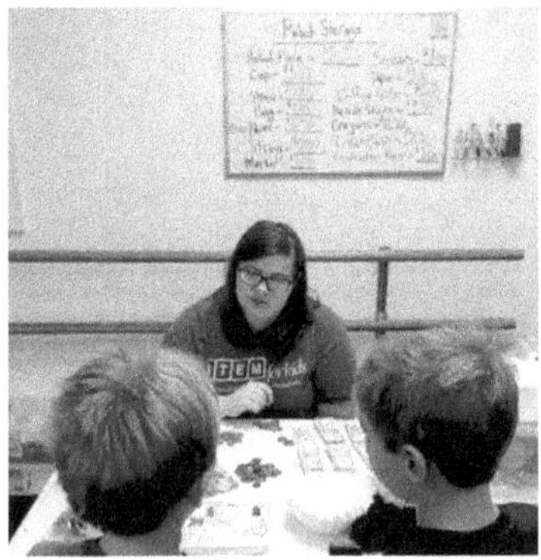

Once the businesses are all created and the STEM Store is set up, you can now hand them the "My Product" worksheet.

Explain to the participants that they cannot just take materials to build their product for free. They will need to pay for their materials.

Let the participants know that, when we are building projects, we will have to purchase materials to work with. Instead of having the materials out on the table for participants to pick, give each material a cost value.

Hand each participant $20-30 fake dollars. Tell them that they just received a Small Business Grant from the STEM Bank. It is best to use physical bills, even if they are not real. Let them know that they can look at the materials and decide which to buy based on the criteria stated in the activity. They want the product to be stable but affordable.

Note to Coach: The STEM Bank will become important for future sessions as they may use up all their grant money to build their initial products.

Set prices for each material by making materials you think participants would use more and materials you have a lot of cheaper. Let them know that you can change the prices at any time as it will depend on how much we have in stock at our STEM store.

Here is an example of what you can have material prices set to - This includes materials that they can "rent" and exchange later. Remember it comes down to what materials you have available at the STEM Store. Most of these materials were found at dollar stores or amazon.

Material Name	Quantity Purchased	Price Per Quantity
Wooden Piece (Big)	1 piece	$3.00
Wooden Piece (Small)	1 piece	$1.50
Plastic Decor Piece (Small)	1 piece	$1.50
Clothespin	1 clothespin	$0.50
Glass Container (Big) / Plastic Container (Big)	1 container	$5.00
Glass Container (Small) / Plastic Container (Small)	1 container	$3.00
Felt Stickers	1 sticker	$0.50
Rope	6 inches	$2.00
Hoop (Large)	1 hoop	$8.00
Hoop (Medium)	1 hoop	$5.00
Hoop (Small)	1 hoop	$2.00
Leaves	1 leaf	$1.00
Solar Beads	5 beads	$0.50
Styrofoam Ball	1 ball	$2.00
Magnetic Sheet	1 square	$3.00
Magnet	1 magnet	$1.00
Mesh	6 inches	$2.00

Ribbon	6 inches	$1.00
Gem	1 gem	$0.25
Googly Eyes	2 eyes	$0.25
Pom Poms	1 pom pom	$0.25
Straws	1 straw	$0.50
Pipe Cleaners	1 pipe cleaner	$0.50
Popsicle Stick	1 popsicle stick	$1.00
Yarn / String	6 inches	$1.00
Poster Board / Cardstock	1 piece	$3.00
Glitter	1 bottle **RENTED - CAN BE EXCHANGED**	$5.00
Paint	1 bottle **RENTED - CAN BE EXCHANGED**	$5.00
Tape	6 inches	$1.00
Paper / Construction Paper	1 piece	$1.50
Scissors	1 pair **RENTED - CAN BE EXCHANGED**	$1.00
Glue	1 stick **RENTED - CAN BE EXCHANGED**	$3.00
Marker	1 marker **RENTED - CAN BE EXCHANGED**	$1.00
Crayon	1 crayon **RENTED - CAN BE EXCHANGED**	$0.50

See example of pricing sheets below that you can place on the STEM Store materials.

STEM Store Is Open!

STEM *for kids*

Clothespin /
Felt Stickers / Straw
/ Pipe Cleaner
$0.50
1 piece
Glass Container (Big)
$5.00
Glass Container (Small)
$3.00
1 piece

Marker
$1.00
Crayon
$0.50
1 piece - Rented
Can Be Exchanged
Rope / Mesh / Ribbon
/ Yarn / String / Tape
$2.00
6 inches

Hoop (Large)
$8.00
Hoop (Medium)
$5.00
Hoop (Small)
$2.00
1 hoop
Leaves / Magnet /
Popsicle Stick
$1.00
1 piece

Beads
$0.50
5 beads
Balls
$2.00
1 ball
Chalkboard Sheet
$2.00
1 square
Gems / Googly Eyes / Pom Poms
$0.25
1 piece
Scissors / Glue
$1.00
1 piece
Misc Materials
$2.00
1 piece

Have them do the math on how much they owe you and what they should get back. This provides real world practice on conducting mental math.

Participants will need to plan first then buy their materials. Prompt the participants to use the following worksheets to plan, build, and test their product.

How to Price Your Product

Once finished, explain that this activity looked at COGS – Cost of Goods Sold. COGS include the direct cost of materials and the labor that goes into making a product. We just focused on the material costs.

Right now, we understand the direct cost of materials and how it can affect the price of our products. However, before we can start selling, we need to set a price - But how do you know how much to charge?

Here's step-by-step how to decide what price to place on a product:

1. Figure Out the Cost to Make It

   Before setting a price, you need to know how much it costs to make your product. This is called the cost of production.

   Here's what you need to add up:

   - Materials – What do you need to make your product? (Example: Lemons, sugar, cups for lemonade)
   - Labor – If you are spending time making something, your time is worth something, too! (Example: The time you spend squeezing lemons)
   - Other Costs – Anything else needed to make and sell it, like advertising or decorations for your stand.

   Example:
   If it costs you $5 to make 10 cups of lemonade, then the cost for each cup is:

$$\text{Cost per Lemonade} = \frac{\text{Total Cost}}{\text{Number of Lemonades}} = \frac{5}{10} = 50 \text{ cents per cup}$$

2. Now that you know the cost to make the product, you need to set a price that covers your cost and lets you make money.

   You can:

   - Charge a little more than your cost – This helps you make a profit.
   - Think about what customers will pay – If a lemonade stand near you sells lemonade for $1, you might price yours at $1 too.

   Example:
   If you charge $1 per cup of lemonade, but each cup costs $0.50 to make, you are making $0.50 back from the cost of material and an additional $0.50 in revenue!

How to Figure Out Profit and Loss

When participants reach the profit and loss portion of the worksheet, discuss the following information so they can think through their own profit/loss for their products:

Profit is the money you have left over after paying for all your costs.
Loss happens when your costs are more than the money you make.

Profit Formula is as follows that the participants should use for the worksheet:

Profit = Total Money Earned – Total Costs

Example of Profit:

- You sell 10 lemonades at $1 each = $10 earned
- It cost $5 to make them
- Profit = $10 - $5 = $5

Examples of Loss:

- You sell 5 lemonades at $1 each = $5 earned
- But it still cost $5 to make them
- Profit = $5 - $5 = $0 (Break even – no loss, no profit)

- If you only sell 3 lemonades = $3 earned
- $3 - $5 = - $2 (You lost money!)

How to Avoid Loss and Make More Profit?

- Lower your costs – Find cheaper materials.
- Sell at a higher price – But make sure customers are willing to pay!
- Sell more products – The more you sell, the more money you make.

My Product

Keep track of how much you are spending for your product. You need to use 6 materials for your product. If your product is a small item, you must make multiple products for your business. It could be a different design on a current product or a totally different product altogether.

Material	How could you use it in your design?	How many do you need?	Cost	Total Cost
____________			$________	
____________			$________	
____________			$________	
____________			$________	
____________			$________	
____________			$________	

My Cost:

____

Price For Customer:

____

Test Results: *Circle One.*

Quality Check	Has A Unique Feature	Makes A Profit	Profit Made From Customer
Pass / Fail	Pass / Fail	Pass / Fail	$________

3.4 Collecting Taxes

Time Required	**45 - 60 min**
Group Sizes	**1 - 3**
Grade	**K - 8**
Materials Needed	
• STEM Store Set Up • Play Money • Calculators or Paper for Calculations • Envelopes	

Learning Objective

- Understand the concept of sales tax: Participants will be able to explain what sales tax is, why it is collected, and how it helps fund public services like schools, roads, and emergency services.
- Calculate sales tax on purchases: Participants will practice calculating sales tax by applying a given percentage (e.g., 10%) to a purchase total and determining the total cost after tax.
- Recognize the importance of shared responsibility in a community: Through discussion and reflection, participants will explore why taxes are necessary for funding public goods and services, and how taxes benefit both businesses and the broader community.

Ask the participants: Have you ever bought something and had to pay more than the price on the tag? Allow them to share their experiences.

That extra money that was paid is called sales tax. Sales tax is a small amount of money added to the price of things we buy. The store doesn't keep this money - It goes to the government to help pay for things that everyone uses.

Can you think of things in our community that everyone uses and needs? *Schools, roads, parks, libraries, firefighters, hospitals, etc.* Sales tax helps pay for things like new books for the library, fixing roads, paying teachers and firefighters, etc.

Let's say you buy a toy for $5 and the sales tax is 10%. That means you have to pay a little extra - 10% of $5, which is $0.50. So your total cost would be $5.50.

Why do you think the government collects taxes from businesses and shoppers instead of just letting people pay for things like schools and roads on their own? Encourage discussion about fairness, shared responsibility, and helping the community.

Let's practice adding tax to our purchases in our STEM Store while you build your products for your businesses.

Conduct the same steps for the STEM Store - Add a simple tax rate to each full purchase going forward. 10% is great for easy calculations. Demonstrate how to calculate tax for a full purchase.

If I bought 5 popsicle sticks and a pair of scissors, my total cost before sales tax would be $6.00. To calculate the full amount to pay, I would multiply $6.00 by 10% and add that amount to the total cost before sales tax.

$6.00 x 10% = $0.60
$6.00 + $0.60 = $6.60

Have the participants shop for materials and calculate their total price plus tax. They pay the store cashier who collects both the item cost and tax. The store cashier will place the tax collected into an envelope called "Tax Collected." After a while, the Tax Collector (the teacher) will stop by the STEM Store and collect taxes separately.

At the end of the class, the Tax Collector will show the participants the amount of sales tax collected for that particular session. Discuss how taxes could be used in a real-life business or community. Have the participants decide how they would "spend" the collected tax money (e.g. improving the STEM Store, funding a pretend community project...)

See page 117-118 for how to set a price for a product and how to calculate profit and loss.

Ask a few reflection questions:

- Was it easy or hard to add tax to your purchases?
- How did collecting taxes change how much you could buy?
- Why do you think businesses and customers have to pay taxes in real life?
- What would happen if there were no taxes?

My Product with Sales Tax 

Keep track of how much you are spending for your product. You need to use 6 materials for your product. If your product is a small item, you must make multiple products for your business.

It could be a different design on a current product or a totally different product altogether.

Material	How could you use it in your design?	How many do you need?	Cost	Sales Tax	Total Cost
______			$______	$______	
______			$______	$______	
______			$______	$______	
______			$______	$______	
______			$______	$______	
______			$______	$______	

My Cost: ______________

Price For Customer: ______________

Test Results: *Circle One.*

Quality Check	Has A Unique Feature	Makes A Profit	Profit Made From Customer
Pass / Fail	Pass / Fail	Pass / Fail	$______

3.5 Making a Virtual Store

Time Required	60+ min
Group Sizes	1 - 3
Grade	K - 8
Materials Needed	
• Laptop/Projector • Computer per student • Play Money	

Learning Objective

- Understand Business Operations and Team Roles – Participants will learn how businesses function by taking on different roles (owner, employees) and working together to manage a store, source materials, set prices, and sell products in a simulated economy.
- Apply Financial and Resource Management – Participants will practice budgeting, purchasing materials wisely, setting product prices, and handling employee wages, reinforcing real-world concepts of supply, demand, and cost management.
- Develop Critical Thinking and Marketing Skills – Participants will use problem-solving and creativity to build a successful business by designing effective store layouts, developing sales strategies, and implementing marketing campaigns to attract customers.

Explain to the participants that we are going to build a store in Minecraft to sell products to other players. We will need to create the store, find / build the products to sell, and decide on pricing for the products and labor.

Each participant will be given a role in a group of 4. One person will be the owner of the store and the other three will be the employees of the store.

Here is a list of the roles participants can have:

- Owner: You are responsible for the upkeep of the store. You must make sure everyone is fulfilling their responsibilities that work at your store. You help the store wherever needed. You must also pay your employees a certain amount of potato money every 30 minutes.
- Employee: You are responsible for fulfilling the work needing to be done at the store. You make sure either the raw materials are available, the product is made, or your customers are happy. As an employee, you are completing the work that the store needs in order to function.

The worksheet below will help you in deciding roles to give each participant in a group. For any store, they will need three types of employees: Materials Collector, Product Builder, and Sales Person. Write the name of the participant who will hold a certain employee type on the worksheet.

Here is a list of the types of stores they can build and should be written on the top of the worksheet:

- Gem store
- Pickaxe store
- Crafting table store
- A service to the other participants store
- Weapon store
- Armor store
- Bakery store
- Grocery store
- Anything else the groups can think of

Have the participants fill out the worksheet and show you what type of store they are going to build and what type of employee each participant will be. Once approved, they can begin designing their store.

Store Roles

Store Name: ______________________

Type of Store: ______________________

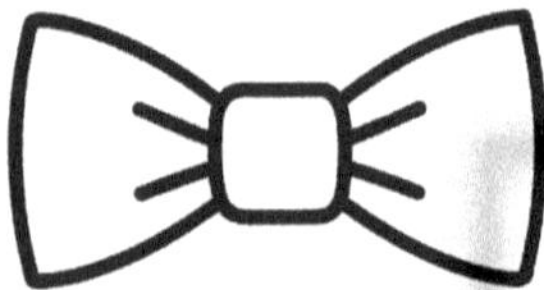 **Owner** ______________ You are responsible for the upkeep of the store. You must make sure everyone is fulfilling their responsibilities that work at your store. You help the store wherever needed. You must also pay your employees a certain amount of potato money every 30 minutes.	 **Materials Collector** ______________ You are responsible for fulfilling the work needing to be done at the store. You make sure either the raw materials are available for the other employee to build the product. As an employee, you are completing the work that the store needs in order to function. You may need to purchase materials from other stores.
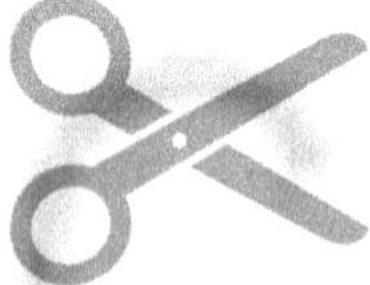 **Product Builder** ______________ You are responsible for fulfilling the work needing to be done at the store. You make sure the product is made to be sold at the store. As an employee, you are completing the work that the store needs in order to function.	 **Sales Person** ______________ You are responsible for fulfilling the work needing to be done at the store. You make sure the customer is happy during the buying process of the product. As an employee, you are completing the work that the store needs in order to function.

Have the participants design the store building with what materials they want to use to make it. Each group will have $100 to spend to make the store.

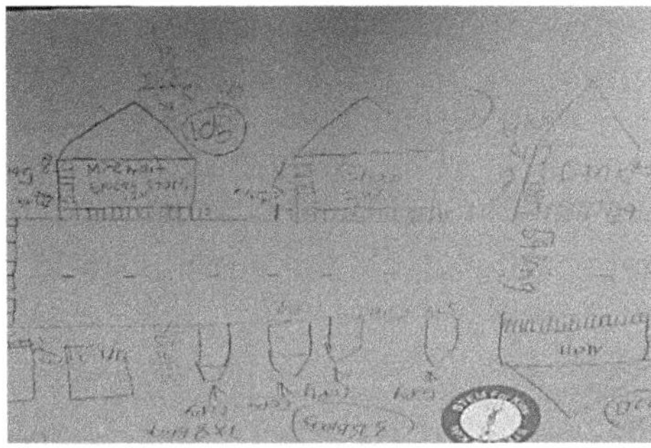

Have the participants draw out a plan on how big the store will be and what materials they will use. Once approved, they can begin building the store building with their budget provided on Minecraft. They will need to make sure the building matches the product they are selling inside and has a sign of the business name on the building.

The only way the participants can get certain materials is by buying the materials from someone called "The Material Contractor." The coach will be the Material Contractor. The Material Contractor can give the participants the materials they want only if the participants send them an email stating what they want, how much they want of that material, and why they need it. Depending on the material, the Material Contractor will let the participant know how much their order is and whether they can get the material.

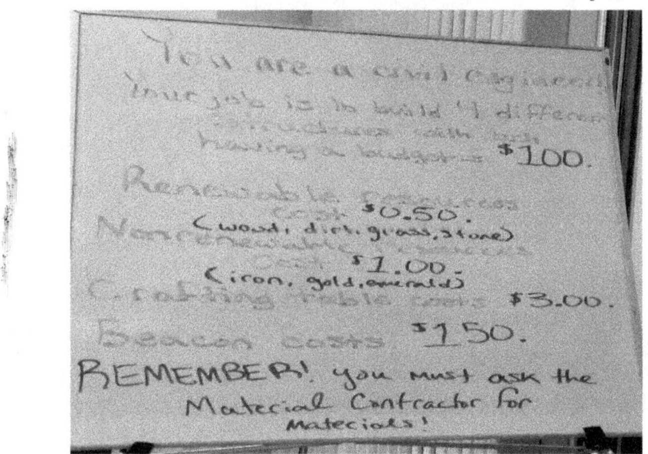

Make sure to have a pricing scale for materials. Renewable resources, or things we can always find more of, will be a low price such as 25 to 50 cents. Nonrenewable resources, or things we have a small supply of, will cost more such as $1 to $1.50. You have the freedom to pick the starting price however you like.

Also, have the option for the participants to buy premade tools (depending on tool, a wooden pickaxe would be $3 but a diamond pickaxe would be more) and crafting tables to save time and money.

For example, say a participant wanted to have 15 wooden blocks and a crafting table. First, the participant would have their budget at hand. Normally, the budget is $100. Renewable resources are priced at $0.50 and nonrenewable resources are priced at $1.00. Crafting tables are $4.00.

Note to Coach: It is a great idea to have artificial currency at hand so that it feels as if the participants are paying for their materials. Make sure to hand different bills out to equal $100.

Using the worksheet, the participant will state which material they would like to buy, how much of that material they would like to buy, why they would like to buy the material, and how much it comes up to.

The example participant would like to buy 15 wooden blocks to make sure the base of the skyscraper they are building is stable and a crafting table to help with creating new tools and technologies with simple materials.

They calculated that the cost would be $11.50. With approval, you can then exchange the money and, using the Give command on the server menu, give the participant the materials they want.

Note to Coach: Participants may ask how much a beacon would be. The price is set for $150 as it helps them move and build faster. Suggest pooling in money with the others in the group for the benefits. You can even have the participants write up a pitch for the whole group.

Note to Coach: Participants will ask you how to make certain items. The following page is a cheat sheet for you with all the recipes for items that we found were important for the projects. Print off this sheet to keep with the coach / kit.

Item Recipe Cheat Sheet

STEM for kids

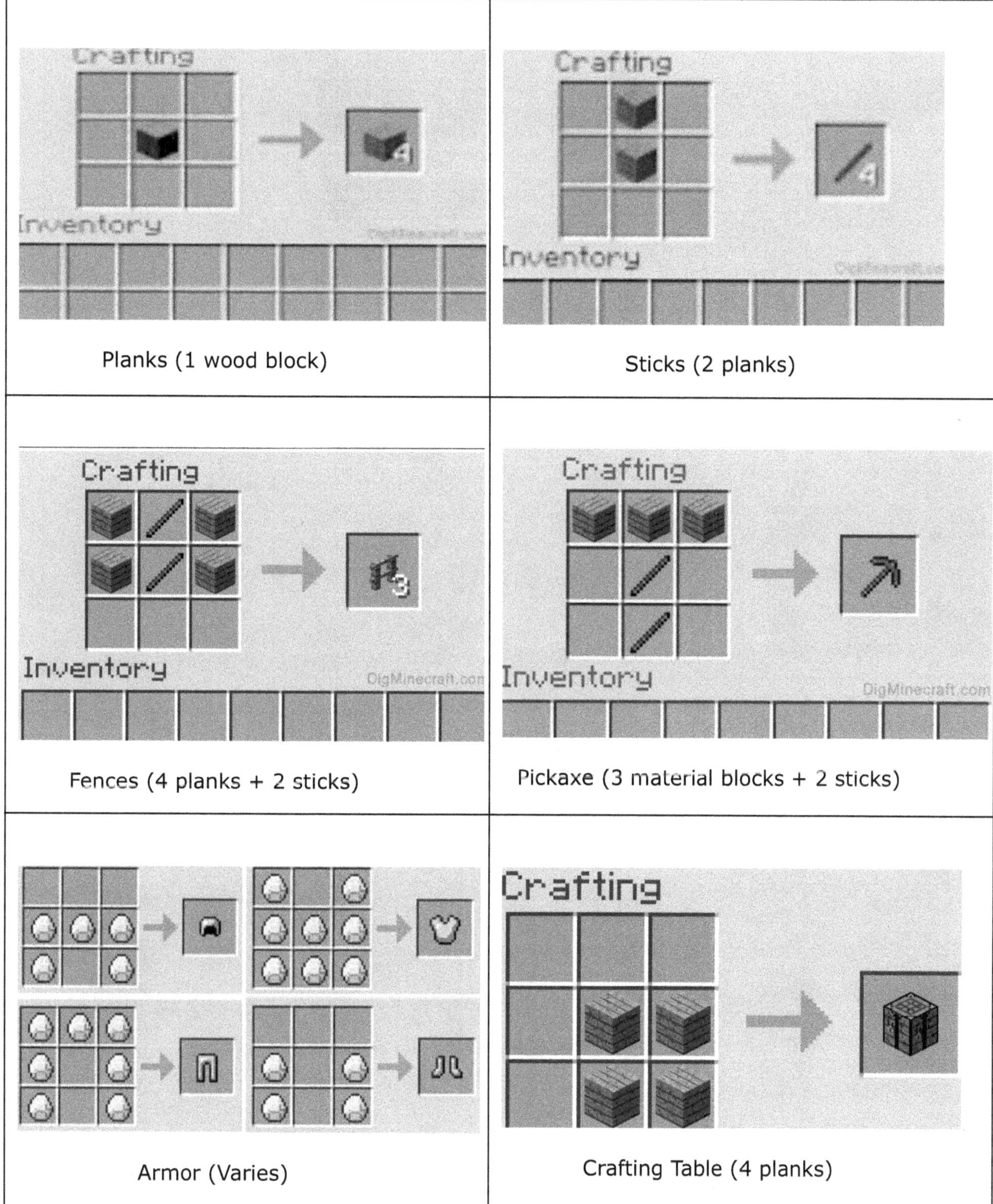

Planks (1 wood block)

Sticks (2 planks)

Fences (4 planks + 2 sticks)

Pickaxe (3 material blocks + 2 sticks)

Armor (Varies)

Crafting Table (4 planks)

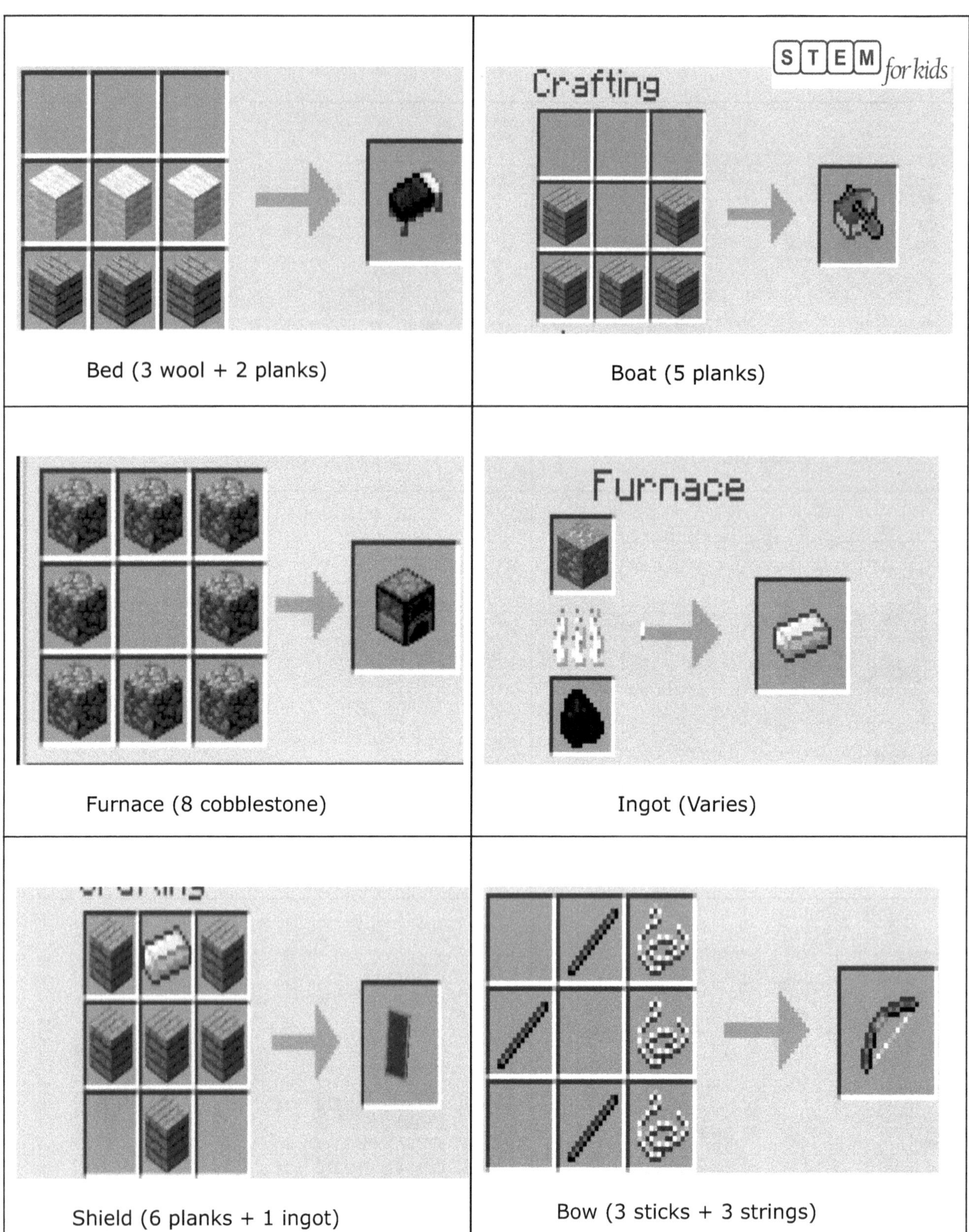

Bed (3 wool + 2 planks)

Boat (5 planks)

Furnace (8 cobblestone)

Ingot (Varies)

Shield (6 planks + 1 ingot)

Bow (3 sticks + 3 strings)

Materials for My Structure

Material Contractor

Materials for My Structure

Dear Material Contractor,

I would like to have ____ amount of ____________________, because ____

____

____

The total price of these materials should be __________.

Thanks,

____

Send   Saved

Materials for My Structure

Material Contractor

Materials for My Structure

Dear Material Contractor,

I would like to have ____ amount of ____________________, because ____

____

____

The total price of these materials should be __________.

Thanks,

____

Send   Saved

Once the store building is ready, the group itself will decide on what products will be sold at the store. They will price the products based on how easy the raw materials are to get and if there are any services associated with it.

Use the worksheet below to decide what products to sell and for how much.

What will You Sell in Your Store?

Use the worksheet to decide what products to sell in your store as well as how much it will cost to get the materials to make the product and what price to place on your product.

Product	How is this Product Unique?	Materials Needed & Prices	Price of the Product

Before building the products to sell at the store, the employees will need to talk with the owner about pay for every 30 minutes of work. No one should be paid above what they would make selling their product for a day.

The employee will create a contract with the worksheet below for how much they will be paid for every 30 minutes they work at the store doing their job. Have the stores open and start at the same time. As the coach, you will keep track of time to let the owner know when to pay their employees for the work they have done.

Owner – Employee Offer Letter

Dear ______________________ ,

I am pleased to offer you a job at ____________________ (name of store), a store that creates / offers

____

____

____

(description of what your store sells).

Your job title will be _______________________________ .

You will be paid _______________ (currency) for every 30 minutes you work at the store.

I am excited to have you onboard at __________________ (name of store).

____________________________________ (signature of owner)

___________________________________ (signature of employee)

Once the store is built, the products are ready, and the employees know their pay, they can open their store to start selling their products. Participants will be given 25 potatoes/emeralds/whatever currency you want as their currency to use in the stores to start with.

Have the participants buy and sell products to each other. Remind them of their jobs that they have and that they need to do their job in order to have money to use.

Note to Coach: If a participant is not following their job responsibilities at a store, explain to them that, in the real world, they could be fired for not helping the store function. Give them a warning to do their job at the store.

Participants can do marketing campaigns to get more customers in their store. They can also create discounts or sales to use on products. Make sure the participants think of creative ways to sell more of their product to other participants.

3.6 Placement for Your Business

Time Required	45 -60 min
Group Sizes	1 - 3
Grade	K - 8
Materials Needed	
• Large Sheets of Paper • Markers and Crayons • Decoration Materials	

Learning Objective

- Understand the Importance of Product Placement – Participants will explore how different products are sold in specific locations and how businesses choose the best places to sell their products, whether in physical stores or online.
- Develop Store Presentation and Marketing Materials – Participants will create essential store materials such as signs and pricing sheets, learning how visual merchandising and clear communication impact customer decisions.
- Apply Marketing Strategies in a Sales Environment – Participants will set up a physical store at the STEM Market, practicing real-world sales techniques and customer engagement to attract buyers and sell their products effectively.

A company needs a product in order to make a profit. Another thing that a company needs is a place to sell that product.

Prompt the participants to think about where they find certain products.

Milk? *Grocery store.*

Wood Planks? *Lowes, hardware stores.*

Computers? *Walmart, online, computer stores.*

Legos? *Lego Store, other stores, online.*

Gas? *Gas stations.*

Certain products are sold in certain places whereas other products can be sold in many places. Explain to the participants that this is the Place for our products to be found. For our product, we will either be placing it at a physical location (like a table during a STEM Market where parents, teachers, admin, or other students can go to and buy products from these businesses) or on a website for customers to buy it from.

Physical Store Location

Have the students know that they will be setting up their store on a table at the STEM Market. They will lay out all their products alongside a store sign and pricing sheets. As they work on building their products, they will need to create these physical materials for the store table.

Note to Coach: You can have the students complete one of these physical materials each class meet up after beginning their product creation. For example, one class could be store sign creation + product creation if they finish their sign. Another class could be pricing sheet fill out + product creation if they finish the pricing sheet worksheet.

Here are examples:

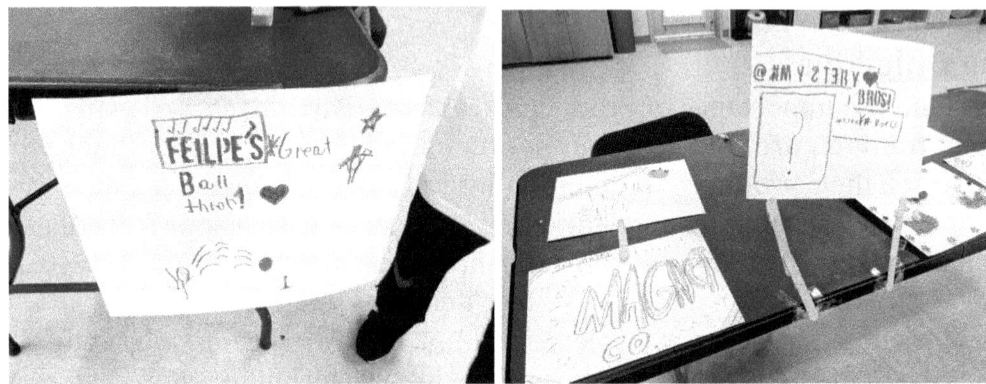

Name of Your Business
NOW OPEN
$
Product 1
Product 2
$
$
Product 3

3.7 Website Design Lab

Time Required	45 - 60+ min
Group Sizes	1 - 2
Grade	2 - 8
Materials Needed	
• Whiteboard/Marker • Laptop/Projector • Computer / Device	

Learning Objective

- Understand the Key Components of an Effective Website – Participants will identify and plan essential website elements, such as product descriptions, pricing, and promotional content, to ensure a user-friendly and informative online presence.
- Develop a Website Blueprint – Participants will use the Website Design worksheet to outline their website structure, determining the layout, images, and information needed to showcase their product effectively.
- Apply Digital Marketing Strategies – Participants will design a website that not only presents their product but also incorporates marketing techniques, such as promotions and advertisements, to attract and engage potential customers.

Now that we have learned about our product and pricing, we will begin designing our own website for the product.

Have the participants think about what they want their website to have on it. Their product will need to be showcased for the customer as well as have information on the product and pricing of the product.

Pass out the Website Design worksheet for the participants to do. The worksheet will help make it clear on what exactly the participant wants in a website.

Note to Coach: Keep this website for the remainder of the program. You will hand this back to the participants every session for them to use when creating their website.

Website Design

Please, fill out the following box in describing what your website will look like. Here is a list description of the objects in the box:

Website Title: The title for your website

Additional Page Names: Everyone will have at least one more page to their website. Think of titles and what these pages will include.

Colors of Website: The colors that your website will be.

Description of Website: A description of the website and what it will be about.

Homepage Title: The title of the homepage for your website.

Body of Homepage: A description of what the homepage will include. You can write out whether there will be pictures in the body, links, drawings, music. Make it detailed as well as you can.

Website Title:

____

Additional Page Names

____

____

Colors of Website:

____

____

Description of Website:

____

____

____

____

Homepage Title:

____

Body of Homepage:

____

____

____

____

____

____

____

____

____

____

____

Participants will need to create a website that showcases their business and products. Whether it is a simple product like a car to a complicated product of a robot, participants will be able to discuss what their product is, what the usage of their product would be, the pricing of the product, and promotions / ads that may go with that product through their website.

Explain to the participants that they will use the following worksheet to make sure they have all the components that they need for a great website for their product. Without these components, customers may not know what the product is, the pricing of the product, or feel the need to get the product.

Website Design Lab Challenge

Tell the participants that they are going to build a website for their business.

1. Go to www.sites.google.com and sign into the Gmail account.
    a. If the participants do not have a Gmail account, provide a STEM For Kids one to use for class.
2. Draw and write out 3 pages that they want to have on their website.
3. Click the "+" on the top left corner of the window.
4. Name your site
    a. Change the Site Document Name by clicking next to the document icon on the top left corner.
        i. This is used for drive organization.
    b. Change the Site Name for your website which appears in the header of the page.
        i. You will need 2 or more pages for your site name to appear.
    c. Change your Page Title by selecting the name of the page.
        i. This will also appear in the navigation menu.

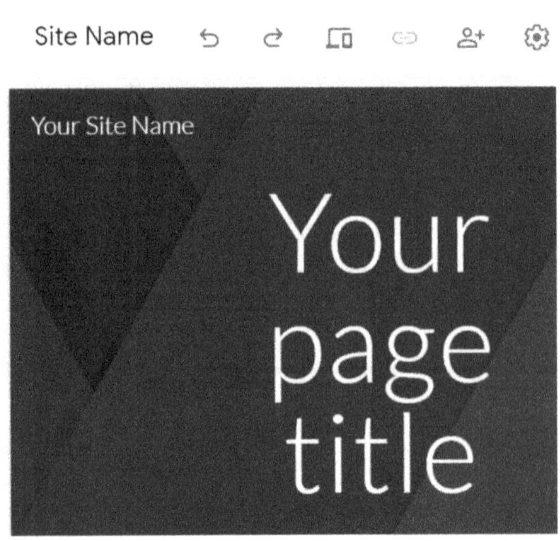

5. Choose a Site Look
    a. Move your mouse to the background image that has the Page Title. You can select a change image and pick an image that suits your website.
        i. Select upload to get an image from your computer or
        ii. Image from gallery to get an image from Google.

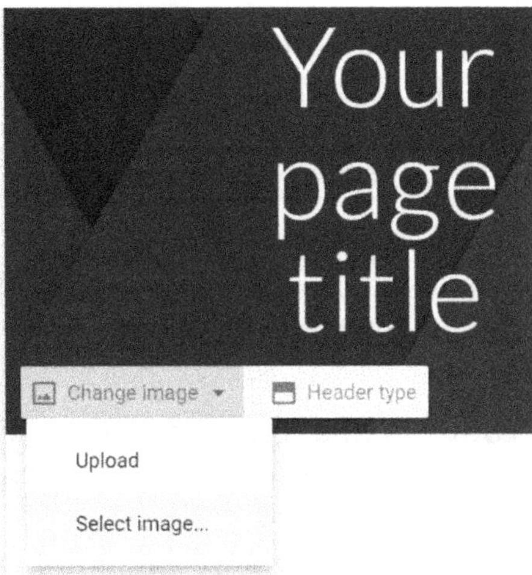

6. You can change the header type to be full sized, banner sized, or nonexistent.
7. Select the THEMES tab on the right side of your website.
    a. You can choose a theme and change the colors/font styles of the theme chosen.

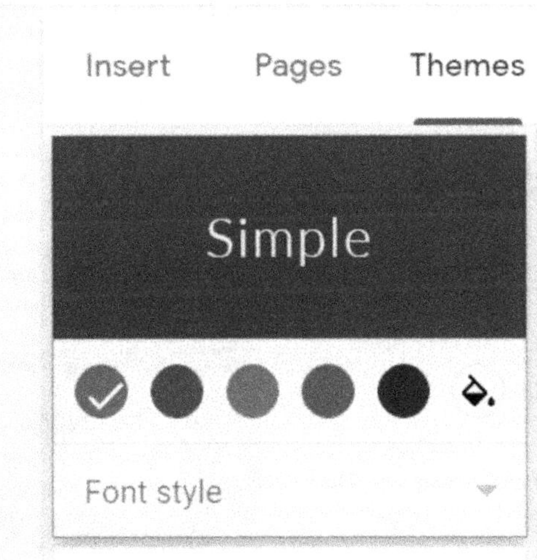

8. Add Content
    a. Double click on the page or go to the INSERT tab on the right of the screen. Click the content you want to add and it will appear on the page.
9. Text
    a. You can add a title and text to any page.
    b. To add text, click the TEXT BOX and it will appear on the page. Enter the text that you want.

c. Use the toolbox to format the text.
d. Change the section color, duplicate text, or reorder the text by clicking on the three icons on the left of the text content.

10. Embed
    a. You can add content directly from the web, such as music and videos.
11. Images
    a. You can add photos, designs, and other images.
    b. To add images, click the IMAGE and it will appear on the page.
    c. To resize, drag the blue dots to the size you want.
    d. You can move the image by clicking the image and dragging it on the image area.
    e. You will see other icons to crop, replace, and add alt text to the image. The icons appear when you click on the image.
12. From Drive
    a. You can add the contents of a folder stored in Google Drive.
13. There are other insert options that you can choose as well.

Let the participants spend a significant amount of time thinking about how they want their website to look. The color and images presented on the website should set the mood on the type of website they are creating. For example, if one was creating a baked goods store website, it would be best to have happy colors like pink and blue.

Now, allow the participants to begin creating their own website. Go around and help if some do not know what exactly they want to do. Allow for a lot of creativity in this activity.

Examples of how a website can look:

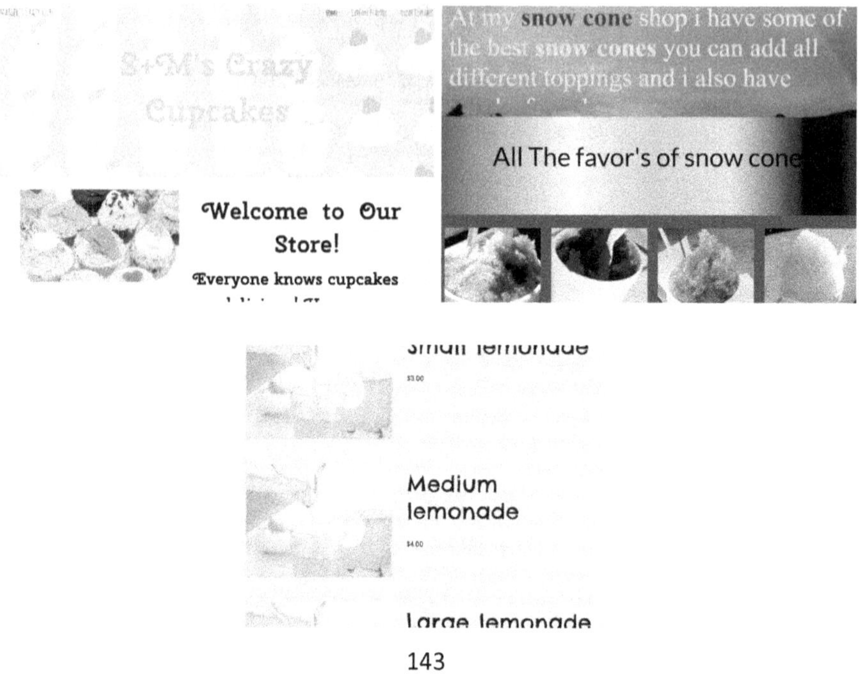

On the Market

Use the worksheet to design a website for your product so that customers can view and purchase it.

Your product: ______________________________

	Description	Check If Finished
Home Page:	Shows the product to the customer. Has a description of the product.	
	Has the logo of your company on the top of the website. Has a marketing message for the product.	
	Has a promotion that the customer can use to purchase the product.	
	Has a clickable picture of the product on the home page and goes to the product page.	
Website:	Has a theme that is appropriate for the product. Text is easily readable.	
Product Page:	Has product pictures for customers to see all parts of the product. Gives description of product to appeal to customers.	
	Explains the components of the product. Lists out what the product is made of and the measurements.	
	Shows pricing of the product. Gives a quantity option. Shows pricing of regular products and additions.	
About Us Page:	Give a short mission statement of your company and why you are behind this product.	
Contact Us Page:	Give a short form for a customer to submit if they have questions.	

3.8 STEM Market

Time Required	30 min
Group Sizes	1 - 3
Grade	K - 8
Materials Needed	
• Whiteboard/Marker • Tables • Table Clothes, optional • All Business Materials & Products • Play Money • Envelopes	

Learning Objective

- Apply math skills to real-world scenarios: Participants will calculate the total cost of items purchased, including sales tax, and determine the correct change to provide customers, reinforcing concepts of addition, multiplication, and basic money management.
- Understand the role of taxes in business and community: Participants will calculate and collect sales tax from customers, place the tax in a designated envelope, and reflect on how sales tax supports public services, developing an understanding of financial responsibility in a community.
- Develop business and customer service skills: Participants will practice setting up and running a business booth, including organizing products, interacting with customers, handling transactions, and using effective communication to ensure a smooth market experience.

Let the participants know that they are going to be opening their businesses to sell their products at the STEM Market! They will set up their booths for their businesses, set up their products in an organized fashion, place their signs, and then open their businesses for customers to come by and purchase their products.

The participants will act as business owners, selling their projects in the market, and calculate total cost of products a customer purchases with tax, collect the money, place the sales tax in a separate envelope titled "Tax Collected, give back the correct change to customers, and provide the tax collected to the Tax Collector at the end of the STEM Market.

Note to Coach: Remind the participants of key concepts of sales tax, total cost with sales tax, and making change before opening the STEM Market. They do not want to be surprised when the Tax Collector comes by for the tax collection!

Follow the steps below to have a successful STEM Market:

1. Organize the tables so that it is easier for customers to go from business to business. Optional: Place table clothes on the tables to make it easier to keep clean and organized.

2. Have each business set up their table for their business. They should display their products and signs. Price tags should be clearly visible.

3. Decide on sales tax (e.g. 10%) and place on the whiteboard the following information:
    a. STEM Market
    b. Remember to:
        i. Add up total cost + sales tax (10%)
        ii. Give correct change
        iii. Place sales tax in the "Tax Collected" envelope
4. Give a small set of play money to each business so they can make change - Between $10-20.

5. Once the businesses are ready, open the STEM Market. This could be a group of students or even families/friends from other classrooms! They should follow the steps below as customers purchase their products from their businesses:
    a. Customer Purchase:
        i. Customers will approach a business, choose an item, and ask the price.
        ii. Business owners will calculate the total cost (price + sales tax) and tell the customer how much they need to pay.
        iii. Business owners will use a calculator to determine the correct sales tax (e.g., 10% of $4.00 = $0.40, so the total price is $4.40).
    b. Money Collection & Change:
        i. The customer will hand over play money or real money for the purchase.
        ii. Business owners will determine the amount of change they need to give back (e.g., customer gives $5.00 for a $4.40 purchase: $5.00 - $4.40 = $0.60 change).
        iii. Use a change-making chart if necessary to assist students in giving the correct change.

c. Tax Collected Per Sale:
    i. After each sale, the business owner will place the collected sales tax into an envelope labeled "Tax Collected."
d. Tax Collection At the End:
    i. The Tax Collector will go around and collect the envelopes with the tax collected.

6. At the end of the STEM Market, have the businesses count out how much money they made at the market. Have them sit in front of the whiteboard to discuss what happened at the Market today. The highlighted questions are great questions to ask in front of families.
    a. Business Ownership and Customer Experience:
        i. How did you feel acting as a business owner? What were the challenges?
        ii. As a customer, did you enjoy buying from other businesses? What did you look for when shopping?
        iii. How did the experience of being a business owner and a customer help you understand how stores work?
    b. Teamwork and Communication:
        i. How did you work with others to make the market run smoothly (as both a customer and a business owner)?
        ii. What was the most fun part of the market? Why?
        iii. How did you communicate with your customers or business owners during the market?
    c. Making Change:
        i. Was it difficult to give the correct change? What made it easier or harder?
        ii. What strategies did you use to make sure you gave the right amount of change?
        iii. How did it feel when you had to handle money and return the correct change to customers?
    d. Sales Tax and Calculations:
        i. Was it easy or hard to calculate the sales tax on your purchases? Why?
        ii. How did you figure out how much sales tax to add to the price?
        iii. What strategies helped you calculate the total cost (item cost + sales tax)?
        iv. How did you feel when you had to make sure the customer paid the right amount, including tax?
    e. Learning About Taxes:
        i. Why do you think the government collects sales tax from businesses and customers?

ii. How could taxes help improve a community or business?
iii. What would happen if there were no sales tax collected? How might it affect the community?

f. Reflection on the STEM Market as a Learning Experience:
   i. How did the STEM Market help you learn about math and money?
   ii. What surprised you most about the experience?
   iii. What would you do differently if we held another STEM Market in the future?
   iv. What did you learn about running a business through this activity?

3.9 Online Money Games

Time Required	30 - 45 min
Group Sizes	1
Grade	2 - 8
Materials Needed	
• Whiteboard / Marker • Computer	

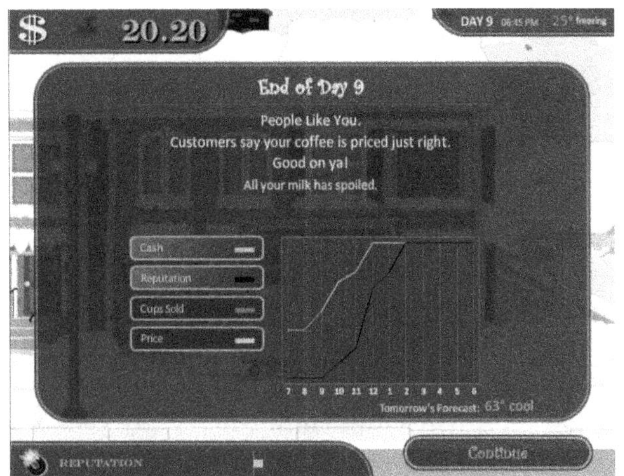

Learning Objective

- Understand how to earn money by selling a product or service.

Now that participants have experienced owning or working at a store, explain that money goes in and out constantly. We have to buy materials and pay employees in order for the store to earn money. Sometimes, this means the profit is less than zero dollars when a store first opens. With time, correct pricing, and reputation, the money earned can increase.

Have the participants play a game called Coffee Shop online.

https://www.coolmathgames.com/0-coffee-shop

This game allows participants to create a recipe for coffee and set the prices of the coffee based on how much they spent on materials. They can also see if customers are enjoying their product or find certain aspects lacking like price or quality.

The participant's goal is to increase their cash in and reputation to the positive. This game shows graphs to explain how well the business is doing.

3.10 Recap

Time Required	15 - 20 min
Group Sizes	1
Grade	K - 8
Materials Needed	
• Paper • Pencil • Whiteboard	

Learning Objective

- Recall and apply terms and ideas related to finance, money, and engineering through an interactive activity.
- Provide an informal opportunity to evaluate participants' comprehension of key topics covered in class.
- Develop the ability to convey and recognize ideas through drawing and verbal explanation.
- Build teamwork and camaraderie by encouraging participants to work together during the game.

For fun, play a game quizzing the participants on whether they truly know the difference between agriculture and horticulture.

Either, the participants can play the game individually (ideally for smaller groups) or in teams of 2-3 with a team name. This will be a buzzer quiz, so once the question has been read, the teams/individuals need to yell out 'buzz' in order to be able to answer.

If correct, they score a point. If not, the remaining players get to answer that question. Once the question has either been answered or no team knows the answer, explain why it is either agriculture or horticulture for that question and move on to the next.

Career Options & Financial Literacy

1. **What factors should you consider when choosing a career?**
    - a) Job responsibilities
    - b) Work hours
    - c) Salary
    - d) All of the above

2. **What does financial literacy help you understand?**
   - a) How to spend all your money
   - b) How to earn money and manage it responsibly
   - c) How to avoid taxes
   - d) None of the above
3. **Which of the following is typically included in a job description?**
   - a) Your salary and work hours
   - b) Your preferred hobbies
   - c) The name of your manager
   - d) Your weekly schedule

Entrepreneurship & Business Planning:

4. **Which of the following is an essential step in creating a business plan?**
   - a) Deciding on a business name
   - b) Ignoring competition
   - c) Choosing your favorite products
   - d) Setting your sales tax rate
5. **What is the role of an entrepreneur?**
   - a) To manage a business and take risks for profit
   - b) To create new products for customers
   - c) To decide how to spend all the business profits
   - d) All of the above

Sales Tax & Financial Responsibility:

6. **What is sales tax?**
   - a) A fee that goes directly to the business
   - b) A percentage of the price of an item that is added and sent to the government
   - c) A type of interest paid on loans
   - d) A discount applied to every purchase
7. **Why is sales tax collected?**
   - a) To increase the business's profits
   - b) To help fund public services like schools and roads
   - c) To give customers a discount
   - d) None of the above
8. **How do you calculate the total cost of an item after adding sales tax?**
   - a) Subtract the sales tax from the original price
   - b) Multiply the original price by the sales tax rate, then add that to the original price
   - c) Add the sales tax to the item price and then subtract the cost of materials
   - d) Multiply the item price by 2

Money Management & Decision-Making:

9. **What is one example of a good decision when managing money?**
   - a) Spending all your money immediately
   - b) Saving money for a larger goal, like buying a new toy
   - c) Ignoring prices when making purchases
   - d) Only spending money on unnecessary items
10. **In a STEM Market, what should you do if a customer gives you more money than the total price of their items?**
    - a) Keep the extra money as a tip
    - b) Return the correct change to the customer
    - c) Add the extra money to your profits
    - d) Ignore the extra money

Customer Engagement & Business Skills:

11. **Why is customer engagement important in a business?**
    - a) To make the customer feel valued and encourage them to buy more
    - b) To ignore the customer and let them figure things out on their own
    - c) To only focus on how much money the business makes
    - d) None of the above
12. **Which of the following would help attract customers to your booth at a market?**
    - a) Displaying your products clearly and neatly
    - b) Ignoring the customers and letting them shop without assistance
    - c) Having no pricing information for your products
    - d) Making your products difficult to see

Since there are multiple answers, you can allow each team to answer the question for points without repeating an answer. Repeating an answer gives a penalty.

Notes

Module 4: Money Smarts

This module teaches essential financial skills through budgeting exercises, real-world simulations, and decision-making challenges. Participants explore managing expenses, taking out loans, evaluating repayment options, and planning for major financial commitments like mortgages and retirement.

Materials

Materials for the Class:

- Whiteboard/Markers
- Laptop/Projector
- Construction Paper
- Markers/Crayons
- Legos of Different Sizes
- Fan
- Table
- Measuring Tape
- Small Toy Animal
- STEM Store
- Balloon/Permanent Marker
- Index Cards
- Bowls

Materials for Each Child/Group:

- Pencil (1 per group / participant)
- Computer (1 per group / participant)
- Recycled Materials ("Treasure Items")
- Engineering Supplies like popsicle sticks, pipe cleaners, straws, string, etc.
- Art Supplies like stickers, washy tape, stamps, pom poms, etc.
- Play Money
- Envelopes
- Dice

4.1 Budgeting My Night Out

Time Required	**30 min**
Group Sizes	**1 class**
Grade	**K - 5**
Materials Needed	
• Whiteboard/Markers • Laptop/Projector	

Learning Objectives for Module

- Practice Budgeting and Financial Decision-Making – Participants will create a budget for a fun evening, making choices based on available funds and prioritizing expenses to stay within their $100 limit.
- Understand Trade-Offs in Financial Planning – Participants will recognize the need to make trade-offs when budgeting, deciding between different entertainment and dining options based on cost and personal preferences.

- Reflect on Real-World Budgeting Challenges – Participants will analyze their budgeting experience, discussing the difficulties of staying within a budget, unexpected costs, and the importance of financial planning in everyday life.

Let the participants know that they are now going to try out a budget on their own. They are going to plan out a fun evening. They can decide on what to do, who they will take with them, and the extras that they will buy.

The participants each have $100 to spend on their fun evening. Explain that each thing they decide to do will be on the whiteboard with prices. Place the table below for the participants to view as they plan their evening.

Things to Do / Buy	Prices Per Person
Movie Ticket	$10
Popcorn	$10
Drink	$4
Candy	$2
Ice Cream	$3
Dinner (Fast Food)	$5
Dinner (Restaurant)	$10

Have the participants use the worksheet below to plan on their fun evening. Let them know that they can bring friends or family along with them on this fun night out.

Prompt the participants to explain what the easiest or hardest things were to do in budgeting a night out. What did they need to keep in mind? Was there anything they could not do that they wanted to do? Budgeting keeps us within the amount of money we earn. When we go over our budget, we may have to borrow money which has consequences.

Use the worksheet to plan out your fun evening out.

Budget: $100

Number of People Going Out: _________

Things to Do / Buy	Cost of Things to Do / Buy	Total Cost for Everyone

What were some tradeoffs you had to make in order to stay within budget?

____

____

____

4.2 Making a Budget

Time Required	20 min
Group Sizes	1 class
Grade	K - 8
Materials Needed	
• Whiteboard/Markers • Laptop/Projector	

Learning Objective

- Understand the purpose of a budget and how it helps manage income and expenses.
- Learn to track earnings and spending to determine if there is enough money for desired purchases.
- Develop decision-making skills by creating a budget for a given scenario and identifying necessary adjustments.

Ask the participants if they have ever seen their parents work on a budget for spending for a month. Maybe they are writing down all the programs the participant is involved with like dance, art, or STEM, alongside the price of that program.

A budget is an estimate of income and spending for a set period of time. If a person is creating a budget for a month, they are looking at the amount of money they will make within that month and calculating all the spending they will make in that month as well. At the end, they will either see that they will have money left over, just enough money, or not enough money for the month.

A lot of people use budgets to help them control the amount of spending they are doing in a month. If they do not use the budget, they may buy products or services that they do not need which can cause loss of money eventually. We call this loss of money uncontrolled spending.

Let's look at an example budget for a kid!

> If your parents give you $5 a week for allowance, then your "income" or money is $5.
>
> If you want to buy a toy that costs $10, then you know that you do not have enough money yet. You only have $5. Have the participants do the math on how much more money they need to have. $5.

If you save your allowance for two weeks, then you can buy the toy! Have the participants do that math on how much money they would make in 2 weeks.

Now that we know about budgeting for a small item, let's look at a table example with a lot more spending and earning of money. Show participants this example.

Money	**How Much Money Do I Have?**	**How I Got the Money**
Allowance	$5.00	$5 a week for helping my parents
Birthday Money	$10.00	$10 from Grandma
Other Money	$2.00	I found $2 in the sofa!
All Money Together	**$17.00**	**All my money added up**
Things I Want to Buy	**How Much Does It Cost?**	**Why I Want to Buy It**
New Toy	$10.00	I saw it at the toy store and love it!
Birthday Gift for Mom (Ring)	$8.00	Mom would like a ring!
Candy Bar	$1.00	Buy a candy bar at school
What It All Costs	**$19.00**	**Everything I want to buy together**
Do I Have Enough Money? (Money – Cost)	**-$2.00**	**I still need $2.00 in order to buy everything!**

Hand each person a slip of paper with a person on it. They will create a budget for a certain type of person to see if they will have enough money for a week. You can create your own.

Keep Me On Budget!

Use the summary of your character slip to create a budget that they will follow. Decide if the character will be under or over their budget at the end of the week.

One Word Summary of Money	How Much Money Do I Have?	How I Got the Money
All Money Together		**All my money added up**
Things I Want to Buy	**How Much Does It Cost?**	**Why I Want to Buy It**
What It All Costs		
Do I Have Enough Money? (Money – Cost)		

What suggestions would you give your character based on their budget?

____

____

____

____

Character Slips for Budgeting 

Sammy the Squirrel

- **Age**: 9
- **Income**: Sammy sold acorns to other animals in the forest for $10. Sammy helped a neighbor squirrel build a new nest and earned $5. Sammy delivered messages between trees and earned $5.
- **Spending**: Sammy wants to buy a new toy (costs $10), some snacks ($5), and save for a future camping trip ($5).

Bella the Baker

- **Age**: 10
- **Income**: Bella sold cupcakes at the market for $15. Bella baked cookies for a local event and earned $8. Bella taught a class on how to make cupcakes and earned $7.
- **Spending**: Bella needs to buy more flour, sugar, and sprinkles for $10. Bella wants to buy a special treat, like a cupcake from another bakery, for $5. Bella wants to buy a small gift for her friend's birthday for $8.

Timmy the Toy Maker

- **Age**: 8
- **Income**: Timmy sold wooden toy cars and animals for $12. Timmy helped his dad with woodwork and earned $5. Timmy painted pictures of the forest and sold them for $3.
- **Spending**: Timmy buys paint and brushes for $7, buys a gift for a friend ($5), and puts $3 in savings.

Lily the Librarian

- **Age**: 11
- **Income**: Lily earned $10 by shelving books for the week. Lily earned $7 by reading to younger kids at the library. Lily helped organize a book fair and earned $8.
- **Spending**: Lily buys a new book for $8, a snack for $4, and a gift for her sister ($6). She decides to save $5.

Charlie the Chore Champ

- **Age**: 7
- **Income**: Charlie earned $6 by doing chores like cleaning and taking out the trash. Charlie earned $3 by walking a neighbor's dog. Charlie helped rake leaves and earned $4.
- **Spending**: Charlie spends $4 on candy, $7 on a new toy, and saves $3 for a future game.

4.3 Decision Trees & Budgeting

Time Required	30 min
Group Sizes	1
Grade	2 - 8
Materials Needed	
• Whiteboard/Markers • Laptop/Projector	

Learning Objective

- Understand Decision Trees in Budgeting – Participants will learn how decision trees help visualize spending choices and their outcomes, aiding in smarter budgeting.
- Apply Critical Thinking to Financial Decisions – Participants will practice making financial choices, recognizing trade-offs, and prioritizing spending within a set budget.
- Develop Problem-Solving Skills – Participants will create and analyze decision trees for various real-life scenarios, improving their ability to evaluate options and predict financial outcomes.

Many people use decision trees to make decisions on how they want to budget their money. A decision tree is a visual tool that shows different options and their possible outcomes. It looks like a tree with branches that represent different decisions and leaves that show the results of those decisions.

Imagine you are budgeting money for the week. You have choices and each choice leads to different outcomes. A decision tree helps you decide which path to take.

Why do we use a decision tree in budgeting? Here are some reasons:

- **Clarify Choices:** We can see the impact of our choices before making them. If we spend money on one thing, what might we have to give up or change to stay within our budget?
- **Visualize Outcomes:** By drawing a decision tree, we can understand how each decision affects our budget. For example, if we decide to buy a toy, we might not have enough money left for snacks.
- **Practice Making Decisions:** Budgeting often requires trade-offs, and a decision tree shows how each choice leads to different outcomes, helping us learn to prioritize our spending.

Let's work together to make a decision tree. Here are the general steps to creating a decision tree and then we'll create some decision trees for certain characters.

1. Start with a Goal
    a. What do they want to achieve this week?
        i. (e.g., saving money, buying toys, spending on snacks, etc.)

2. Identify Options
    a. What are the possible ways to spend the money?
        i. (e.g., buying snacks, a toy, or saving for a bigger goal)

3. Create the Tree
    a. Draw a simple tree with branches for each decision. Each branch leads to a new set of choices or outcomes
        i. (spending $5 on a toy might leave only $3 for snacks)

4. Evaluate Outcomes
    a. Discuss how each decision impacts their budget.
        i. Does it leave enough for savings? Is it within the weekly allowance?

Here is an example - Draw this decision tree on the whiteboard:

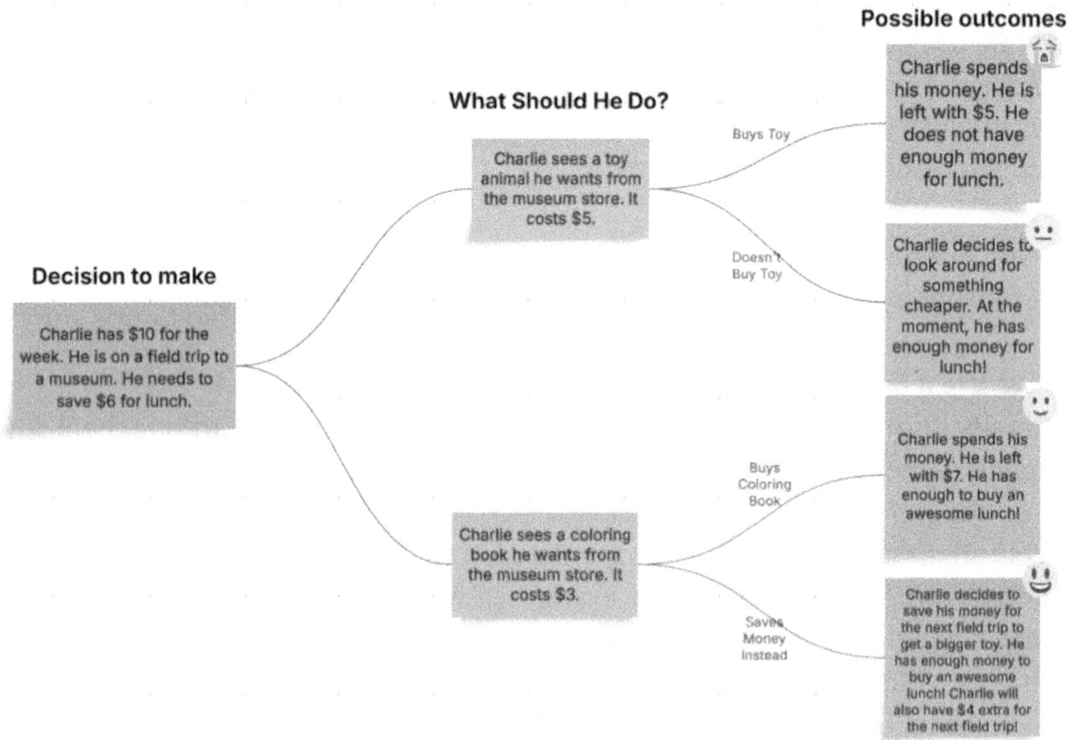

Participants should discuss what will happen if Charlie makes each decision. How does spending on toys affect his ability to buy other things? Can he still save money?

Here are more reflection questions you can ask:

- What happens if you spend all your money on toys? How does that affect your ability to buy other things you want?
- How does saving part of your money now help you in the future? What can you use it for later?
- If you have $10 and need to choose between buying a snack and saving for a future goal, what might you do? Why?

We can use decision trees to make decisions for many different scenarios. Here are a few scenarios that you can give to each participant to complete a decision tree using the template worksheet below.

- Problem: Choosing the best deal at a grocery store.
    - Decision points: Price, quantity, quality, brand.
- Problem: Planning a budget for a school trip.
    - Decision points: Transportation, accommodations, activities, food.
- Problem: Identifying an unknown animal.
    - Decision points: Habitat, characteristics (e.g., fur, feathers, scales), diet.
- Problem: Selecting the best plant for a garden.
    - Decision points: Sunlight requirements, water needs, soil type, climate.
- Problem: Choosing a college major.
    - Decision points: Interests, skills, career goals, salary potential.
- Problem: Debugging a computer program.
    - Decision points: Error messages, code analysis, testing.
- Problem: Designing a website.
    - Decision points: Purpose of the website, target audience, content, layout.

My Decision Tree

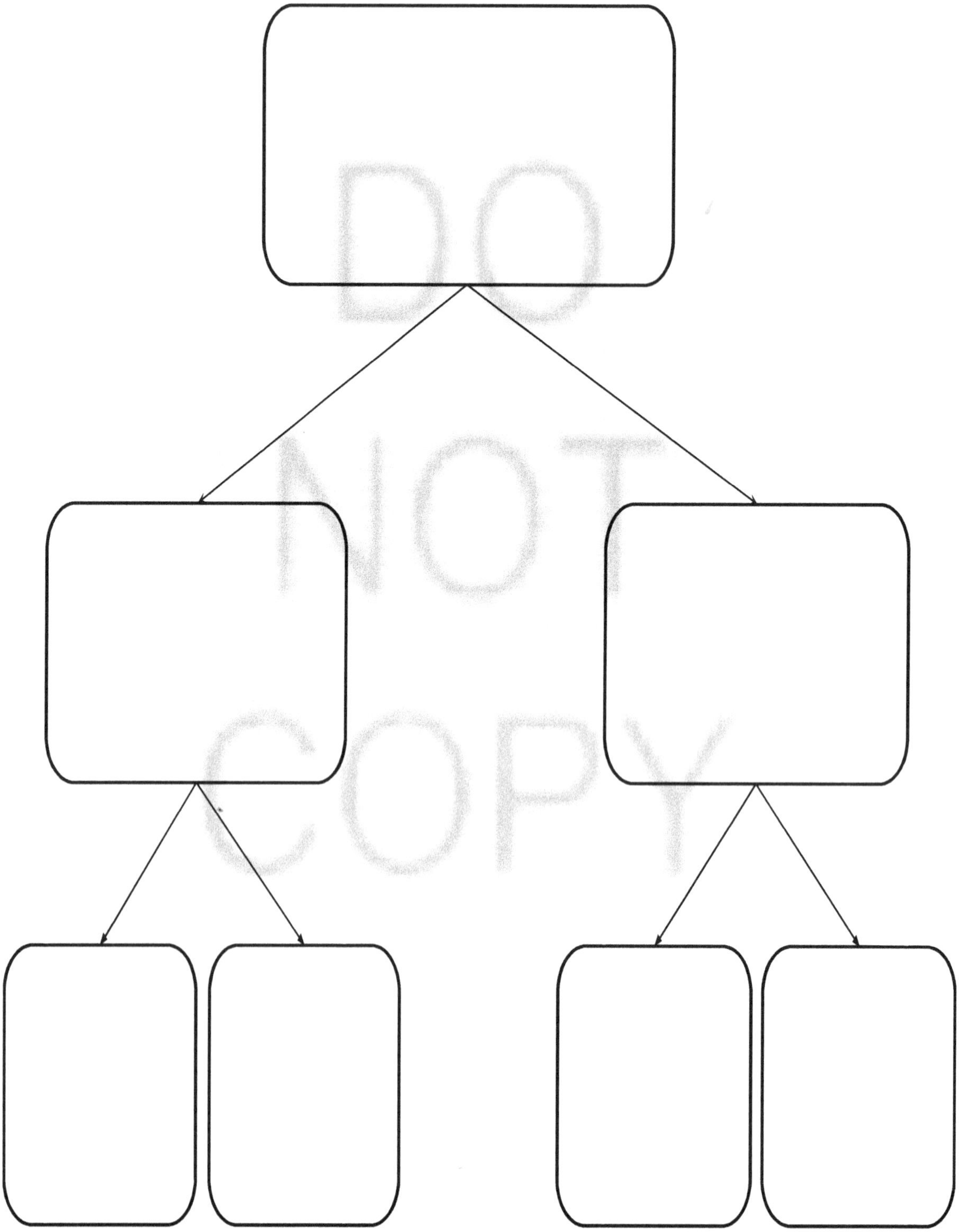

4.4 Engineering Budget Challenge

Time Required	45 - 60 min
Group Sizes	1
Grade	K - 8
Materials Needed	
• Whiteboard/Markers • Laptop/Projector • Legos of Different Sizes • Fan • Table • Measuring Tape • Small Toy Animal	

Learning Objective

- Apply Budgeting Strategies – Students will create and manage a budget, prioritizing material purchases to build a stable skyscraper while staying within financial constraints.
- Utilize the Engineering Design Process – Students will follow the engineering design process to plan, construct, and test a skyscraper that meets specific criteria and constraints.
- Analyze Trade-offs in Decision-Making – Students will evaluate how different material choices impact cost, strength, and stability, making strategic trade-offs to optimize their design.

We are going to take on the role of engineers and city planners! Your challenge is to design and build a skyscraper using Legos, but just like in real life, you will have a budget to manage. Every project has a budget—whether it's building a house, a bridge, or even planning a school event. A budget is a plan for how much money you have and how you will spend it wisely.

Why is budgeting important?

- It helps us make smart choices with our money.
- It ensures we have enough resources to complete our project.
- It teaches us to prioritize what we need versus what we want.

You will have $400 to buy materials for your skyscraper. Different Lego pieces have different costs, so you'll need to plan carefully. If you spend all your money too quickly, you may not have enough to complete your structure. But if you budget wisely, you can build a strong skyscraper that meets all the requirements!

Before you start building, you'll plan your design and budget by choosing the right materials. Think about:

- How many pieces you'll need.
- Whether large or small Lego blocks are better for your design.
- How to make your skyscraper strong while staying within your budget.

Just like real engineers, you will face challenges and trade-offs—do you spend more on larger blocks for strength or save money for extra pieces? Will your design stay under budget while still meeting all the criteria? Remember, good budgeting leads to a successful project! Using the Engineering Design Process, the goal is to make a skyscraper using legos. Facilitate the discussion.

Criteria:

- The skyscraper must hold its own weight.
- It must hold a live weight (the small stuffed toy).
- It must withstand a wind test (from the fan).
- It must withstand an earthquake (shaking the table).
- It must be free-standing.

Constraints:

- Use only legos
- Each small lego block costs $5
- Each large lego block costs $10
- All other lego pieces cost $7
- You have $400 budget to make your skyscraper

Test:

- Hold the live weight for 10 seconds
- Wind test
- Earthquake test
- Measure height

Handout the "Skyscraper Design Challenge" worksheet. Let participants ask questions and plan their skyscrapers. Encourage them to draw their ideas. Have them think in 3D – many times children start thinking about their plans in 2D. Remind them that they need to build behind the one side that they are drawing and that they need to account material for that too.

Check their plans, have them think through material planning especially to stay within the budget targets. Once the plans seem roughly ok, have them "purchase materials." Keep a tally of how much they have spent and how much is left in their budget. Participants should keep track of their budget.

Older kids should also maintain their own tally; help younger children through math.
If issues arise over similar designs, use the STEM for Kids' patents.

My Engineering Design Process

Did it work?
YES: How can it be better?
NO: How can we fix it?

What do we have to work with and what do we want it to do?

Improve

Ask

The Goal:

What have we learned to complete this challenge?

Create

Imagine

Build it!

Plan

Draw out a few ideas on how to complete this challenge:

My Engineering Design Plan

Material	Properties	How could you use it in your design?

Draw a possible solution:

Skyscraper Design Challenge

Material	How Can You Use It In Your Design?	How Many Do You Need?	Cost	Overall Total Cost
Small Lego Block			$5	
Large Lego Block			$10	
Other Lego Pieces			$7	

My Cost: ____________

Draw a diagram:

Test Results: *Circle One.*

Dead Load	Live Load	Wind	Earthquake	Height	Cost
Pass / Fail	Pass / Fail	Pass / Fail	Pass / Fail		

4.5 Budgeting Application Analysis

Time Required	30 - 45 min
Group Sizes	1
Grade	3 - 8
Materials Needed	
• Whiteboard/Markers • Laptop/Projector • Device for each participant	

Learning Objective

- Apply Budgeting Principles – Students will calculate their monthly take-home pay, allocate expenses, and determine savings, learning to manage a budget effectively.
- Analyze Salary Growth and Inflation – Students will forecast their salary and expenses over 15 years, considering annual salary growth and inflation to understand long-term financial planning.
- Develop Problem-Solving and Coding Skills – Students will use Python to model financial scenarios, analyze data, and answer financial questions, reinforcing computational thinking and data analysis.

Let the participants know that they just got a new job to work as a data analyst. They want to budget all their living expenses based on their salary. They need to keep in mind the expenses they need monthly, taxes, salary growth over time, and inflation for all expenses.

Note to Coach: You can use any software that allows you to code in Python. You may need to test your software first to be sure the code will work. The screenshots below use IntelliJ software. Another great web-based tool is https://trinket.io/ - You just need to have an account for students to use.

Their budget will have to keep in mind the following:

- Rent
- Food expenses
- Entertainment expenses
- Emergency fund

As a data scientist, they are going to be working at a technology company in New York City. Their starting salary will be $85,000 per year. After state and local taxes, they are expected to send roughly 30% back to the government each year.

Note to Coach: There are activities on taxes in Module 3 of this curriculum. Explain that taxes are money taken out of what people earn / spend to help society raise money to cover public costs like parks or their school.

Before they can calculate their budgeting, participants will need to calculate their monthly take home pay after taxes.

```
In [1]: salary = 85000
        tax_rate = 0.3
```

```
In [2]: salary_after_taxes = (salary * (1 - tax_rate))
        print("Salary after taxes: " + str(round(salary_after_taxes, 2)))

        Salary after taxes: 59500.0
```

```
In [3]: monthly_takehome_salary = (salary_after_taxes / 12)
        print("Monthly takehome salary: " + str(round(monthly_takehome_salary, 2)))

        Monthly takehome salary: 4958.33
```

In[1]: This line creates a variable for salary which is set at 85,000. This line creates a variable for the tax rate which is set at 0.3. This is calculated by dividing 30 by 100 to move it from a percentage.

In[2]: This line calculates the salary after taxes for a full year. This line prints the salary after taxes for a year. The number '2' refers to how many places past the decimal the program should show. When dealing with money, we only need to show the hundredth place. The answer is $59,500.

In[3]: This line divides the salary after taxes by 12 in order to get the monthly salary return. This line prints out the monthly salary return. The answer is $4,958.33.

Let the participants know that they have decided to split a two-bedroom apartment with a friend. They will need to budget for rent, food, and entertainment. They also want to make sure they have money aside for emergencies. The money for emergencies could be used for anything ranging from new clothes or electronics to doctor appointments.

They will need to budget for the following:

- Rent - $1200 / month (This includes utilities)
- Food - $30 / day

- Entertainment - $200 / month
- Emergencies - $250 / month

The participants will need to calculate their monthly expenses. Whatever is left after paying the monthly expenses will go into their savings account. They will need to calculate their monthly savings as well.

Assume that there is an average of 30 days per month.

In [4]:
```
monthly_rent = 1200
daily_food_budget = 30
monthly_food_budget = 900
monthly_entertainment_budget = 200
monthly_emergencies_budget = 250
```

In [5]:
```
monthly_expenses = (monthly_rent + monthly_food_budget + monthly_entertainment_budget + monthly_emergencies_budget)
print("Monthly expenses: " + str(round(monthly_expenses, 2)))
```

```
Monthly expenses: 2550
```

In [6]:
```
monthly_savings = monthly_takehome_salary - monthly_expenses
print("Monthly savings: " + str(round(monthly_savings, 2)))
```

```
Monthly savings: 2408.33
```

In[4]: These lines set variables for each expense type that needs to be budgeted.

In[5]: This line creates the function to find out how much the monthly expenses are. This line prints the monthly expenses amount out. The answer is $2,550.

In[6]: This line creates the function for how much will go into monthly savings. This line prints out the amount. The answer is $2,408.33.

As a data analyst, the participants want to understand how much they could make staying at this job over years.

The participants can expect their salary to grow at different rates depending on their job. Since they are working in a growing and in-demand career field, they can assume a steady growth in their annual salary.

Assume an annual salary growth rate of 5%. Basic math tells us that, if we start at $85,000 per year, we should expect to earn over $176,000 per year after 15 years. After taxes, assuming our rate is still 30%, we should take home roughly $125,000 per year.

Have the participants figure out the monthly salary growth and then figure out the actual salary forecast over time.

In [7]:
```
import numpy as np
```

In [8]:
```
forecast_months = 12*15
annual_salary_growth = 0.05
```

In [9]:
```
monthly_salary_growth = (1+annual_salary_growth)**(1/12) - 1
```

In [10]:
```
cumulative_salary_growth_forecast = np.cumprod(np.repeat(1 + monthly_salary_growth, forecast_months))
```

In [11]:
```
salary_forecast = monthly_takehome_salary*cumulative_salary_growth_forecast
```

In[7]: This line imports NumPy.

In[8]: This line creates a variable that finds the amount of months in 15 years. This line sets the annual salary growth rate by dividing the percentage by 100.

In[9]: This line calculates the monthly salary growth rate.

In[10]: This line forecasts the growth of their salary.

In[11]: This line calculates the actual salary forecast by using the current monthly salary return.

In [21]:
```
import matplotlib.pyplot as plt
```

In [22]:
```
plt.plot(salary_forecast, color='blue')
plt.show()
```

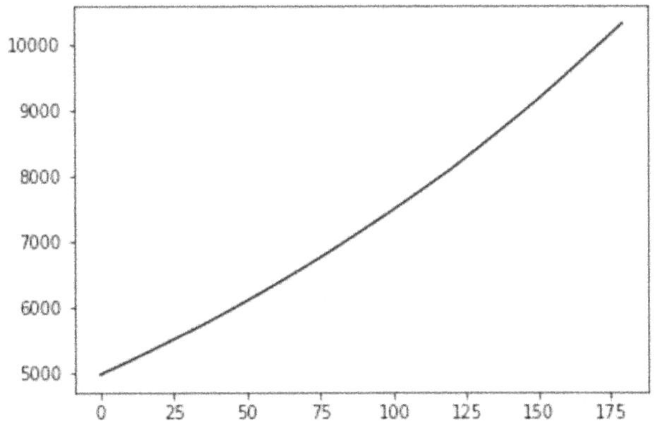

In[12]: These lines import matplotlib and the inline libraries for graphing.

In[13]: This line plots the salary forecast to the number of months up to 15 years. This line shows the graph.

Not only will the participants need to worry about how much money they will make in 15 years, they will need to understand how their expenses may rise due to the inflation. This can impact how much they put into savings!

Participants need to also assume that their monthly expenses will rise by an average of 2.5% per year due to inflation. This means that there will be a higher cost of living over time. Luckily, their salary is growing faster than inflation, so this means they should have more money going into savings each month.

They will need to figure out their monthly expenses by adjusting for growth due to inflation.

```
In [23]: annual_inflation = 0.025

In [24]: monthly_inflation = (1+annual_inflation)**(1/12) - 1

In [25]: cumulative_inflation_forecast = np.cumprod(np.repeat(1 + monthly_inflation, forecast_months))

In [26]: expenses_forecast = monthly_expenses*cumulative_inflation_forecast
```

In[14]: This line sets the annual inflation variable to 0.025 which is the 2.5% divided by 100.

In[15]: This line changes the annual inflation variable to reflect the inflation per month.

In[16]: This line forecasts inflation over time.

In[17]: This line calculates the forecasted expenses over time.

In [28]:
```
plt.plot(expenses_forecast, color='red')
plt.show()
```

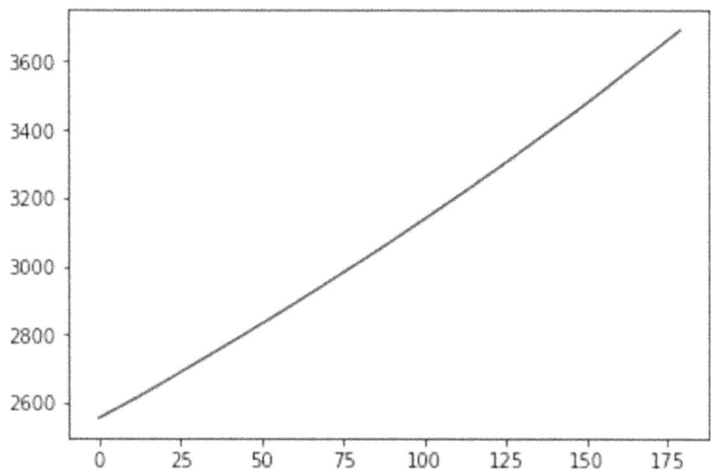

In[18]: These lines plot a graph for the monthly expenses over time due to inflation.

Once participants have calculated their monthly salary, monthly expenses, forecast salary up to 15 years, and forecast expenses up to 15 years, they will need to answer a few questions that they may have about their finances in the future.

The questions can be answered in many ways which means there is no correct answer for the participants to follow. Use what you know to get the answers.

Have the participants open a note pad file on the laptop and type out the following questions we want to answer based on the data:

Specific Questions

- Using what you know about your monthly salary and expenses, imagine that a new expense occurs that must be done monthly: Credit Card Bill. Your credit card bill is $64 per month. Calculate what your monthly expenses would be. How much would you be able to save now?
- You have decided to pick up a part time job at a local grocery store. The job pays you $10 an hour to work 15 hours a week. You know that 20% of your paycheck goes back to the government due to taxes. Calculate what your monthly salary would be totaling both your full and part time jobs. Figure out how much you would save each month with the additional paychecks each month.

Broad Questions

- What sort of suggestions would you give yourself to save more money each month?

- Based on the analysis, look at the average salary for your dream job and use the monthly expenses from the project above. Figure out the monthly salary, monthly savings, forecasted salary, and forecasted savings for your dream job.

Once participants have written out the questions for them to answer, they may begin to do so on python. They should start with one question and show proof of their answer.

You may use the examples above to stir them in the correct way but allow the participants to come up with their own solutions.

Salary Data Analysis

Specific Questions

- Using what you know about your monthly salary and expenses, imagine that a new expense occurs that must be done monthly: Credit Card Bill. Your credit card bill is $64 per month. Calculate what your monthly expenses would be. How much would you be able to save now?

- You have decided to pick up a part time job at a local grocery store. The job pays you $10 an hour to work 15 hours a week. You know that 20% of your paycheck goes back to the government due to taxes. Calculate what your monthly salary would be totaling both your full and part time jobs. Figure out how much you would save each month with the additional paychecks each month.

Broad Questions

- What sort of suggestions would you give yourself to save more money each month?

- Based on the analysis, look at the average salary for your dream job and use the monthly expenses from the project above. Figure out the monthly salary, monthly savings, forecasted salary, and forecasted savings for your dream job.

4.6 Taking Out a Loan

Time Required	45 - 60 min
Group Sizes	1 - 2
Grade	K - 8
Materials Needed	
• Whiteboard/Markers • Laptop/Projector • Legos of Different Sizes • Fan • Table • Measuring Tape • Small Toy Animal	

Learning Objective

- Apply Budgeting and Financial Decision-Making – Students will manage a set budget, determine the cost of materials, and decide how to best allocate resources while constructing a stable bridge.
- Understand the Concept of Loans and Interest – Students will explore how loans work, including how interest is calculated and the impact of repayment periods on total loan costs.
- Evaluate Risk and Rewards of Financial Choices – Students will analyze loan options and justify their decision based on long-term financial impact.

A loan is money that you borrow from a bank or lender with the promise to pay it back over time. But banks don't lend money for free—they charge something called interest. Interest is the extra money you pay on top of the amount you borrowed.

For example, imagine you borrow $10 from a friend and they say, "You have to pay me back $12 next week." That extra $2 is the interest or cost of borrowing money.

The amount of interest depends on two things:

- Interest Rate – The percentage the bank charges for lending you money.
- Loan Term – The number of months or years you have to pay it back.

Why Do People and Businesses Take Loans?

- To buy expensive things like houses, cars, or even start a business.
- To cover unexpected costs, like medical emergencies or project delays.
- To invest in something that will grow over time, like education or new technology.

How to Evaluate a Loan

Before taking a loan, you should ask these important questions:

1. **How Much Money Am I Borrowing?**
   This is called the loan amount or principal. If you need $200 to build your dream home, the loan amount is $200.

2. **What is the Interest Rate?**
   The interest rate tells you how much extra you have to pay back.
   It is written as a percentage (%).
   - A lower interest rate means you pay back less extra money.
   - A higher interest rate means you pay back more extra money.

   Example:
   - Loan 1: $100 loan with 5% interest → You pay back $105
   - Loan 2: $100 loan with 10% interest → You pay back $110
   - Which one is better?
     - Loan 1! It has less interest.

3. **How Long Do I Have to Pay It Back?**
   This is called the loan term.
   (how many months or years you have to repay the loan)
   - Short-term loans = Higher monthly payments, but you finish paying faster.
   - Long-term loans = Lower monthly payments, but you pay more interest over time.

   Example:
   - Loan 1: Pay $50 per month for 2 months (faster)
   - Loan 2: Pay $25 per month for 4 months (slower)
   - Which one is better?
     - It depends! If you want to finish paying quickly, Loan 1 is better. If you need smaller payments, Loan 2 is better.

4. **What is My Monthly Payment?**
   The monthly payment is how much money you have to pay every month. You want to make sure it's something you can afford!

   Rule of Thumb:
   - A good loan should have a monthly payment that is 30% or less of your take-home pay.

Comparing Loans – Example

Let's say you are choosing between two loans - Write on the whiteboard and follow along doing the math with the participants:

Loan Option	Loan Amount	Interest Rate	Loan Term	Monthly Payment	Total Payback
Loan 1	$200	5%	2 months	$105 per month	$210
Loan 2	$200	3%	4 months	$52 per month	$208

Which one is better? Have the participants make decisions first before giving any answers.

- Loan 1: You finish paying faster but have higher monthly payments.
- Loan 2: You pay slightly less overall and have lower monthly payments.

If you can afford the higher payments, Loan 1 helps you finish paying quicker.
If you need smaller payments, Loan 2 is better.

Smart Loan Decisions

Summarize with the participants about steps for smart loan decisions:

- Pick a loan with low interest
- Choose a loan with payments you can afford
- Try to pay it off as soon as possible to avoid too much interest
- Compare different loan options before making a decision

Loans for Construction

Imagine you are an engineer working on a major construction project. You've carefully planned your bridge, budgeted your materials, and started building. But suddenly, an unexpected problem arises! Maybe you need extra support to make the bridge stronger, or bad weather has caused delays, and you now have additional costs. What do you do if you don't have enough money left?

This is a common challenge in the real world. Companies, engineers, and even individuals sometimes need more money than they currently have to complete a project or handle an emergency. That's where bank loans come in!

- As you build your bridge, an emergency will occur that requires extra funding. You'll have to decide whether to take out a loan from The Bank of STEM to complete your project. But be careful! Different loans have different terms, and some may cost more in the long run than others.

Using the Engineering Design Process, the goal is to make a bridge using legos. Facilitate the discussion.

Criteria:

- The bridge must hold its own weight.
- It must hold a live weight (the small stuffed toy).
- It must withstand a wind test (from the fan).
- It must withstand an earthquake (shaking the table).

Constraints:

- Use only legos
- Each small lego block costs $5
- Each large lego block costs $10
- All other lego pieces cost $7
- You have $400 budget to make your skyscraper

Test:

- Hold the live weight for 10 seconds
- Wind test
- Earthquake test
- Measure length

Handout the "Bridge Design Challenge" worksheet. Let children ask questions and plan their bridges. Encourage them to draw their ideas. Have them think in 3D – many times children start thinking about their plans in 2D. Remind them that they need to build behind the one side that they are drawing and that they need to account material for that too.

Check their plans, have them think through material planning especially to stay within the budget targets. Once the plans seem roughly ok, have them "purchase materials." Keep a tally of how much they have spent and how much is left from "The Bank of STEM."

Older kids should also maintain their own tally; help younger children through math.

If issues arise over similar designs, use the STEM for Kids' patents.

My Engineering Design Process

Did it work?
YES: How can it be better?
NO: How can we fix it?

What do we have to work with and what do we want it to do?

Improve

Ask

The Goal:

What have we learned to complete this challenge?

Create

Imagine

Build it!

Plan

Draw out a few ideas on how to complete this challenge:

My Engineering Design Plan

Material	Properties	How could you use it in your design?

Draw a possible solution:

Bridge Design Challenge

Material	How Can You Use It In Your Design?	How Many Do You Need?	Cost	Overall Total Cost
Small Lego Block				
Large Lego Block				
Other Lego Pieces				

My Cost: ____________

Draw a diagram:

Test Results: *Circle One.*

Dead Load	Live Load	Wind	Earthquake	Height	Cost
Pass / Fail	Pass / Fail	Pass / Fail	Pass / Fail		

In the middle of the groups building the bridge, explain that an emergency has occurred where they have more money going out than what they have currently. Pick the amount based on how much the group has left. You can be detailed on what emergency occurred for each group.

Here are some examples of emergencies you can use:

- Material Shortage
    - While constructing the bridge, they realize they don't have enough Lego pieces to make it stable. They need to buy more materials to reinforce the structure.
    - Cost: $50-$100

- Structural Weakness Discovered
    - During a routine check, the bridge shows signs of instability and needs additional support to prevent collapse.
    - The team must purchase extra materials to strengthen key areas.
    - Cost: $75-$100

- New Safety Regulations
    - A "government official" (teacher) announces a new safety law requiring all bridges to be at least 10 inches wide to handle future traffic loads.
    - The team must expand their bridge, requiring more materials.
    - Cost: $50-$100

- Unexpected Earthquake Damage
    - The team was testing their bridge when a sudden "unexpected earthquake" (shaking the table) caused damage, requiring urgent repairs.
    - To meet the challenge's criteria, they must buy extra reinforcement materials.
    - Cost: $75-$100

- Increased Weight Requirement
    - Engineers realize the bridge will need to hold a heavier live weight (add an extra small stuffed animal).
    - To prevent collapse, the team must strengthen the structure with additional Lego blocks.
    - Cost: $50-$100

- Fast-Track Construction Order
    - A "client" (teacher) demands that the project be completed earlier than expected.
    - To finish on time, the team must pay for premium materials that allow for faster assembly.
    - Cost: $75-$100

Explain that they need to have more money to afford the cost of the emergency. Luckily, the STEM Bank is offering personal loans!

Loans are money that is borrowed, especially a sum of money that is expected to be paid back with interest. Interest is money paid back at a particular rate for the use of that money lent.

Write on the whiteboard 2 loan options the participants can choose from. Participants will need to decide which loan is the best option by figuring out how much they would have to pay each month and how much interest they would give back to the STEM Bank overall.

- Loan of $100. Interest rate of 12%. Must be paid in 12 months.
- Loan of $100. Interest rate of 5%. Must be paid in 6 months.

Once the group has chosen which loan they will go with, have them sign a piece of paper stating the loan they will take. Give them the money.

At the end of the activity, have the participants explain which loan they thought was the best and give reasons why. Explain that each loan has risks and rewards. It depends on the group on which works best for them at the time.

STEM Bank: Business Loan Application

Business Profile

____

Business Name

____

____

____

Business Owner(s)

____

State

In what month and year did you start the business?

____

Type of Business Entity:

- ▢ Sole Proprietorship *(By Yourself)*
- ▢ Limited Liability Co. *(L.L.C.)*
- ▢ Partnership *(With Partner)*
- ▢ Corporation *(Co.)*

Loan Request

I/We, individually and/or on behalf of the business, hereby apply to STEM Bank for a loan:

$ __________________________

Amount Requested (Between $30 to $50)

Purpose for Loan:

- ▢ Working Capital *(Paying Employees)*
- ▢ Real Estate *(Location / Office)*
- ▢ Equipment / Material Purchase
- ▢ Vehicle Purchase *(Car)*

Provide more details on why you need this loan amount - <u>STEM Bank can refuse approval based on reasoning</u>:

____

____

____

____

____

____

____

____

____

Sticker of Approval From STEM Bank:	**Signatures of Approved Business Owner(s):**

4.7 My New Construction Home EDP

Time Required	60+ min
Group Sizes	1
Grade	3 - 8
Materials Needed	
• Whiteboard/Markers • Laptop/Projector • Recycled Materials ("Treasure Items") • Engineering Supplies like popsicle sticks, pipe cleaners, straws, string, etc. • Art Supplies like stickers, washy tape, stamps, pom poms, etc. • Anything else you think they would love to build with • Play Money • STEM Store	

Learning Objective

- Apply financial literacy skills by creating a budget, selecting a mortgage loan, and evaluating the affordability of homeownership based on income and expenses.
- Use engineering principles to design and construct a structurally sound home model that meets specific criteria, including stability, durability, and functionality.
- Develop problem-solving and critical thinking skills by making informed trade-offs in home design, adjusting financial plans, and improving structural integrity based on test results.

Congratulations! You've been working hard and saving money for years, and now it's time to take a big step—building your dream home from the ground up. Unlike buying an existing home, a new construction home allows you to design everything from the layout and number of rooms to special features like a garage, backyard, or even a pool. However, building a house comes with important decisions, especially when it comes to financing your home.

Most people don't have enough cash to pay for a house upfront, which is why they take out a mortgage loan. A mortgage is a type of loan used to buy or build a house, where the bank lends you money, and you agree to pay it back over time with interest. If you don't make your payments, the bank has the right to take back the house—so choosing the right mortgage is an important financial decision!

In this project, you will take on the role of an architect, engineer, and financial planner to design and build a new home while staying within a budget.

You will need to complete the following Project Phases:

- **Design Phase:** Sketch your home layout through a blueprint while following project criteria for rooms and extras.
- **Budgeting Phase:** Assign costs to each element of the home and calculate your total cost, ensuring you stay within the initial budget of $100.
- **Mortgage Selection:** Once the initial budget is used, choose from different mortgage loan options to complete the new construction build and use formulas to calculate your monthly payments.
- **Final Presentation:** Present your home design, explain your budgeting choices, and discuss your mortgage selection.

By the end of this project, you'll have a fully designed home model and a mortgage plan, just like real homeowners and builders do. But remember—just like in the real world, unexpected costs may arise, and you'll need to make smart financial choices!

Engineering Design Project: My New Construction Home

Goal: Ask the participants what is an acceptable goal for building a house. Make sure they realize that they need to think about what the house will be able to do once built and add that to the goal.

Build a new house with all the rooms and features you want while staying within your budget and choosing the best mortgage to pay for it.

Ask/Imagine Stage: Have the participants ask questions about the project. You should answer questions on what materials they can use, the criteria for the project, any constraints they may have with the project, and how they can test the project and know if it works or does not work.

Build a new house with all the rooms and features you want while staying within your budget out of materials provided:

- Recyclable Materials (Like bottle caps, aluminum foil, parchment paper, newspaper, etc.)
- Decorating supplies like stickers, gems, glitter, etc.
- Engineering Supplies like popsicle sticks, pipe cleaners, straws, string, etc.
- Art Supplies like washy tape, stamps, pom poms, different paper, etc.
- Anything else you think they would love to build with

Materials to help build but will not be used as part of your design.

- Tape, scissors, crayons, markers, glue, etc.

Explain when engineers work their supplies are limited, so they have to plan for a small amount of supplies.

Criteria:

- The house must include 3 bedrooms, 2 bathrooms, 1 kitchen + dining spot, and 1 living area.
- The house must have a stable structure that can stand on its own. This includes a strong foundation, sturdy roof, and a window in each room for fire safety.
- The design must fit within the given land space.
- The house must include at least one additional feature (e.g., a deck, garage, or backyard).
- The final design must be presented with a floor plan and cost breakdown.

Constraints:

- Use only the materials as specified.
- The house must fit within the designated plot size.
- The design must be structurally sound and able to stand on its own.
- The number of rooms and features must stay within the budgeted cost.
- The total construction cost must not exceed $1,000.
- A mortgage loan must be selected to cover any costs beyond the initial budget of $100.
- The monthly mortgage payment must be calculated and fit within an affordable range of your salary.
- The monthly mortgage payment cannot exceed a reasonable percentage of income, typically 30% or less.

Test:

- Check if the total construction cost stays within the assigned budget.
- Verify that the selected mortgage plan allows for affordable monthly payments.
- Ensure the house structure stands on its own without collapsing.
- Assess whether the final construction meets the initial design plan and criteria.
- Calculate the total loan repayment amount and compare it with the budgeted financial plan.

Plan

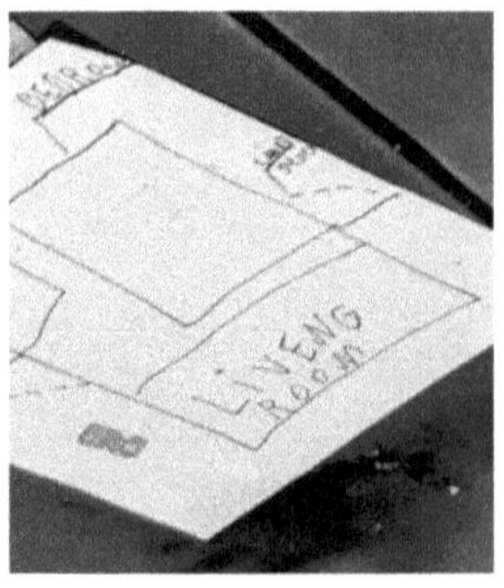

For the Plan section, you will have the participants create a blueprint for their home. Have the participants draw out the floor plan for their home. You can ask engagement questions like: What features would you want in a dream home? What factors do you think affect the cost of a home?

They should have the following showing on the plan: 3 bedrooms, 2 bathrooms, 1 kitchen + dining spot, and 1 living area; a strong foundation, sturdy roof, and a window in each room for fire safety; at least one additional feature (e.g., a deck, garage, or backyard). The final plan must be presented with a floor plan and cost breakdown as best as they can.

Make sure the participants note down the materials they are using, how much material they are using, and how they plan to use each material. Help participants weigh their wants vs. needs in home construction. Guide them in understanding financial trade-offs (e.g., a bigger house means higher costs).

Once participants have completed their plan, they must seek approval from the teacher before beginning to build. You can use a sticker or a simple check mark to write on their plan as approval. Confirm that all required rooms and features (e.g., bedrooms, bathrooms, kitchen, deck, yard) are included in the design. Review the blueprint to make sure the house fits within the given plot size.

Note to Coach: For younger groups, use the next activity to simplify this project.

Extension: Insulation – Participants can explore the importance of insulation in maintaining energy efficiency and temperature control within their homes. They can research different types of insulation materials, their costs, and their impact on heating and cooling expenses, then decide how to incorporate insulation into their home design while staying within budget.

Extension: Plumbing – This extension introduces participants to the basics of home plumbing, including water supply and drainage systems. They can plan and budget for necessary plumbing fixtures like sinks, toilets, and showers while considering water conservation techniques, costs, and the impact of plumbing decisions on home functionality.

Extension: HVAC – Participants will learn about heating, ventilation, and air conditioning (HVAC) systems and their role in maintaining indoor air quality and comfort. They can research different HVAC options, compare costs and energy efficiency, and integrate a system into their home design while ensuring affordability.

Extension: Electricity – This extension focuses on electrical planning, where participants will design an electrical layout for their home, considering outlets, lighting, and appliances. They will explore the costs of wiring, safety precautions, and how energy-efficient choices can impact their monthly utility expenses.

My Engineering Design Process

Did it work?
YES: How can it be better?
NO: How can we fix it?

What do we have to work with and what do we want it to do?

Improve

Ask

The Goal:

What have we learned to complete this challenge?

Create

Imagine

Build it!

Plan

Draw out a few ideas on how to complete this challenge:

My Engineering Design Plan

Material	Properties	How could you use it in your design?

Draw a possible solution:

My Home Blueprint

STEM for kids

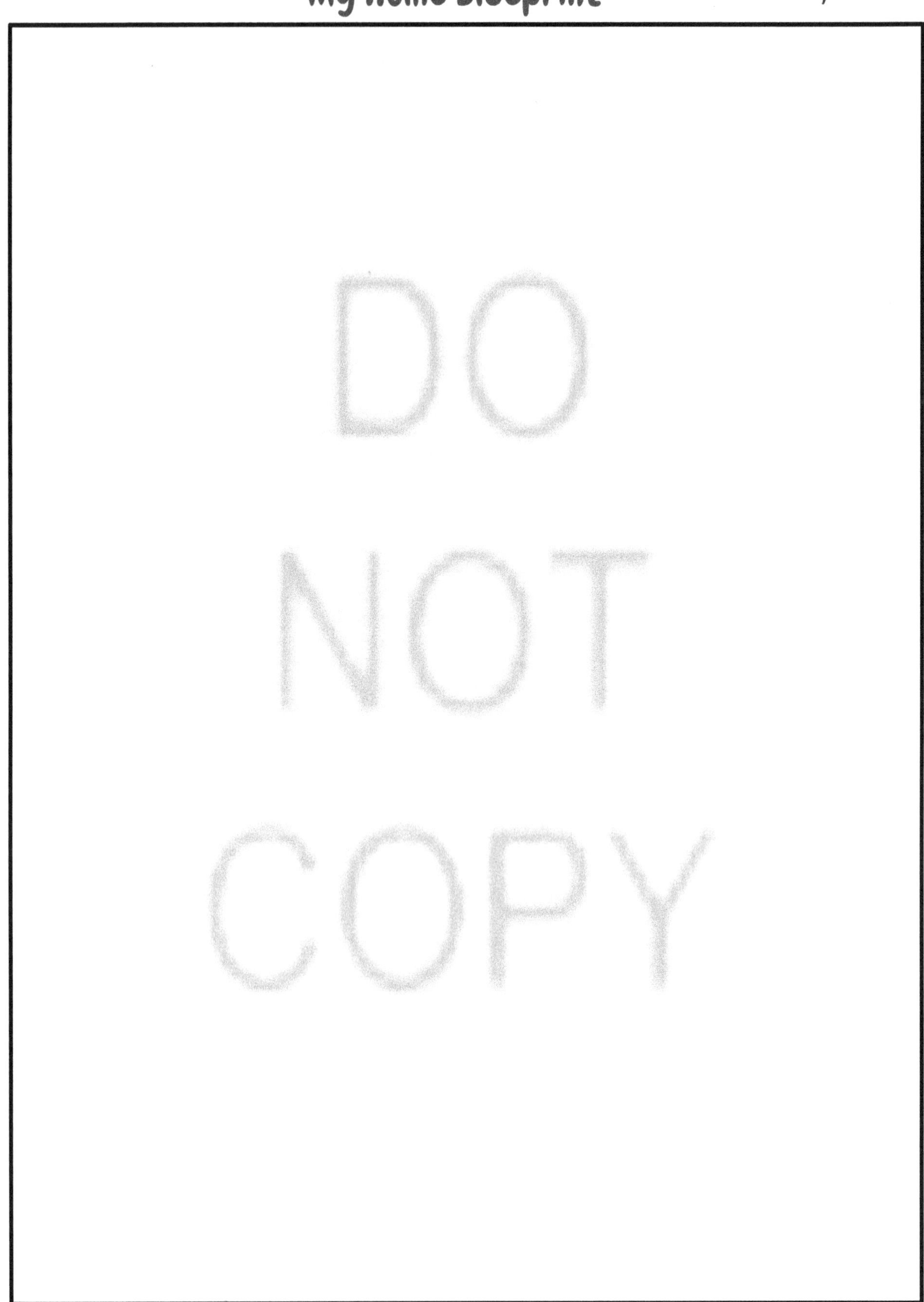

Build

Set up the STEM Store - You can find the instructions in Module 3 Activity 3 of this course. Only follow the instructions for setting up the STEM Store and purchasing.

Allow participants to construct their home model. They should purchase the materials they want with the play money provided. They should bring their blueprints to life by constructing a 3D model of their home. They should consider the structure stability, room arrangement, and proportionality. Encourage them to be creative - They should add windows, doors, and furniture details.

Make sure participants track their spending on the budget worksheet. Each room and additional feature has a cost. They should ensure that they stay within their budget. If they exceed their budget, the participants will need to adjust their design or apply for a mortgage loan to cover the extra costs.

The mortgage loan requires an application to the STEM Bank where it will be reviewed if they can afford the mortgage loan of their choice. If they cannot afford the loan with their salary, the application will be denied and they can try again with a different mortgage loan.

Participants must complete the following for the mortgage loan application:

- Select a career and use the provided salary to calculate the monthly income (divide annual salary by 12).

- Compare the income with the mortgage payment to determine if the loan is affordable based on standard financial guidelines.
    - Housing costs should not exceed 30% of monthly income.

- Adjust the application based on down payment (money put down from current savings) and mortgage terms (each loan will have a certain term) to see how different financial decisions impact affordability.

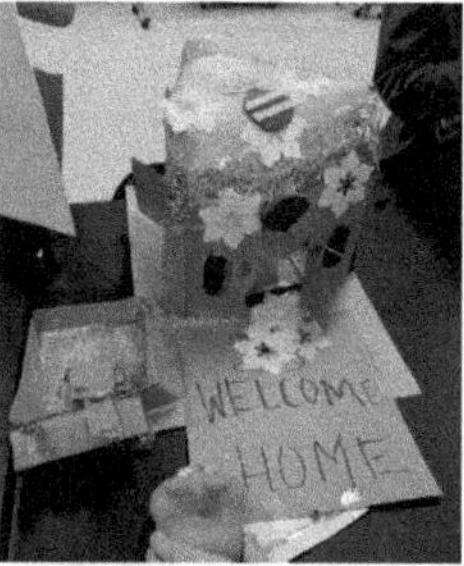

Keep Me On Budget!

Use this worksheet to keep track of your purchases from the STEM Store.

Initial Budget: _________

Mortgage Loan Budget: _________

Material Bought	Full Cost	What Will It Be Used For?
What It All Costs		
Do I Have Enough Money? (Money – Cost)		

My Salary

Have the participants scale down the amount of money for the classroom by dividing the amounts by 1,000.

Teacher – $60,000 per year or $ ________ Current Savings: $30,000 or $________
Lawyer – $150,000 per year or $________ Current Savings: $120,000 or $________
Construction Manager – $95,000 per year Current Savings: $60,000
Software Engineer – $120,000 per year or $________ Current Savings: $80,000 or $________
Graphic Designer – $65,000 per year or $________ Current Savings: $30,000 or $________
Nurse – $75,000 per year or $________ Current Savings: $40,000 or $________
Electrician – $68,000 per year or $________ Current Savings: $35,000 or $________
Marketing Specialist – $72,000 per year or $________ Current Savings: $50,000 or $________
Dentist – $160,000 per year or $________ Current Savings: $130,000 or $________

Chef – \$70,000 per year or \$ ________ Current Savings: \$35,000 or \$________
Retail Store Manager – \$100,000 per year or \$ ________ Current Savings: \$50,000 or \$________
Data Analyst – \$90,000 per year or \$ ________ Current Savings: \$55,000 or \$________
Social Worker – \$58,000 per year or \$ ________ Current Savings: \$20,000 or \$________
Pharmacist – \$130,000 per year or \$ ________ Current Savings: \$115,000 or \$________
Architect – \$80,000 per year or \$ ________ Current Savings: \$45,000 or \$________
Accountant – \$78,000 per year or \$ ________ Current Savings: \$45,000 or \$________
Pilot – \$110,000 per year or \$ ________ Current Savings: \$75,000 or \$________
Mechanical Engineer – \$85,000 per year or \$ ________ Current Savings: \$100,000 or \$________

Home Mortgage Loans

Pick a mortgage loan to complete the mortgage application. Currently, the mortgage loans are set just like they would be in the real world. When receiving the money from the loan for classroom use, remember to scale down the amount of money by dividing the amounts by 1,000. Do your math on the back of this page.

Standard Construction Loan Loan Amount: $200,000 Interest Rate: 5% Loan Term: 15 years	**Flexible Home Loan** Loan Amount: $300,000 Interest Rate: $4% Loan Term: 30 years
Short-Term Home Loan Loan Amount: $350,000 Interest Rate: 3% Loan Term: 15 years	**Extended Loan** Loan Amount: $250,000 Interest Rate: 6% Loan Term: 30 years
Small Business Construction Loan Loan Amount: $50,000 Interest Rate: 6% Loan Term: 15 years	**Mini Loan** Loan Amount: $25,000 Interest Rate: 10% Loan Term: 15 years

Which loan will you choose for your project? Why?

___

___

___

How will the loan amount and repayment terms affect how you spend on materials?

___

___

___

Will you need to make sacrifices to your blueprint? Any challenges you'll face?

___

___

___

Home Mortgage Application

Personal Information

Name: ______________________________

Age: _________

Grade: _________

Date: _____________________________

Project Details

Total Cost of Your Home Construction (from the Budget Worksheet):

____

Down Payment From Savings:

____

Amount You Need to Borrow (Loan Amount):

____

(Loan Amount = Total Cost - Down Payment)

Your Mortgage Loan Request

☐ **Standard Construction Loan**: $200,000, 5% Interest, 15 Years Term

☐ **Flexible Home Loan**: $300,000, 4% Interest, 30 Years Term

☐ **Short-Term Home Loan**: $350,000, 3% Interest, 15 Years Term

☐ **Extended Loan Option**: $250,000, 6% Interest, 30 YearsTerm

☐ **Business Construction Loan**: $50,000, 6% Interest, 15 Years Term

☐ **Mini Loan**: $25,000, 10% Interest, 15 Years Term

Approved

Loan Details

Now, let's calculate the monthly payments and interest. This will help you understand how much you'll need to pay back monthly.

Loan Amount: ________________________

Interest Rate: ________________________

Loan Terms (Months): _________________

- Interest Amount = _________________

  (Interest = Loan Amount x Interest Rate)

- Total Loan Repayment = ____________

  (Total Repayment = Loan Amount + Interest)

- Monthly Payment: _________________

  (Monthly Payment = Total Repayment / Loan Term)

Is Your Monthly Payment Affordable?

A smart mortgage choice means making sure your payment is not more than 30% of your monthly take-home salary.

Monthly Take-Home Salary: ___________

30% of Your Monthly Salary: __________

(Affordable Limit = Monthly Salary x 0.30)

Is your mortgage 30% or less of your salary?

Yes No

Loan Agreement

By signing below, you agree to use your mortgage loan responsibly and repay it according to the terms of your chosen loan. You understand that you need to make monthly payments, and you are committed to completing your home construction project within the given budget.

____

Applicant's Signature

____

Date

Test

Once construction is complete, have the participants test the integrity of their houses:

- **Weight Test** – Place a small weighted object (such as a small toy) on the roof to see if it can support additional load without collapsing.
- **Wind Test** – Use a fan or blow air at the house to simulate strong winds and check if it remains standing.
- **Shake Test** (Earthquake Simulation) – Gently shake the surface the house is built on to see if the structure remains intact.
- **Waterproofing Test** – Lightly spray or drip water onto the roof and walls to check if there are leaks (simulating rain conditions).
- **Foundation Strength Test** – Apply light pressure on different sides of the house to see if it tilts or collapses, ensuring a strong base.
- **Door and Window Stability Test** – If students include doors and windows in their design, check if they function properly without breaking or causing the structure to weaken.

Improve

After testing the structural integrity of their homes, participants should analyze what worked well and what could be improved. Encourage them to reflect on the test results and make modifications to strengthen their designs.

Ways to Improve:

- **Reinforce Weak Areas** – If the home failed the weight or shake test, consider adding extra supports or a stronger foundation.
- **Improve Wind Resistance** – Adjust the roof angle or add stabilizing features to withstand wind forces.
- **Enhance Waterproofing** – Use different materials or design features like sloped roofs to prevent leaks.
- **Optimize Space Usage** – Reevaluate room layouts to ensure an efficient and functional home design.
- **Budget Adjustments** – If over budget, find ways to reduce costs without compromising structure, such as choosing different materials.

Encourage participants to apply these improvements and retest their homes to see if their modifications make a difference!

Reflection

Participants should now have a physical model of their home and a financial breakdown of their construction choices. Allow the participants to reflect on their project by testing their knowledge of budgeting and mortgage loan impacts on home ownership.

Ways to reflect on the home build project:

- **Group Discussion** – Have participants share what went well, what challenges they faced, and how they overcame them.
- **Budget Review** – Reflect on whether they stayed within budget and how financial decisions impacted their home design.
- **Mortgage Affordability** – Analyze if their chosen salary could realistically support their mortgage payments and overall expenses.
- **Engineering Design Reflection** – Discuss how the engineering design process helped improve their home's structure and functionality.
- **Testing Results** – Review how well their home withstood the structural tests and what design elements contributed to its success or failure.
- **Personal Takeaways** – Write or discuss what they learned about budgeting, mortgages, home construction, and problem-solving.
- **Improvement Brainstorm** – Think about what they would change if they could rebuild their home with a new approach or budget.
- **Career Connection** – Reflect on how engineers, architects, and financial planners use these concepts in real-world home construction.

Encourage participants to document their reflections in a journal, group presentation, or classroom discussion!

4.8 STEM For Tots™: My New Construction Home EDP

Time Required	60+ min
Group Sizes	1
Grade	PreK - 1
Materials Needed	
• Whiteboard/Markers • Laptop/Projector • Recycled Materials ("Treasure Items") • Engineering Supplies like popsicle sticks, pipe cleaners, straws, string, etc. • Art Supplies like stickers, washy tape, stamps, pom poms, etc. • Anything else you think they would love to build with	

Learning Objective

- Apply financial literacy skills by creating a budget and learning about loans.
- Use engineering principles to design and construct a structurally sound home model that meets specific criteria, including stability, durability, and functionality.
- Develop problem-solving and critical thinking skills by making informed trade-offs in home design on budget and improving structural integrity based on test results.

Congratulations! You've been working hard and saving money for years, and now it's time to take a big step—building your dream home from the ground up. Unlike buying an existing home, a new construction home allows you to design everything from the layout and number of rooms to special features like a garage, backyard, or even a pool. However, building a house comes with important decisions, especially when it comes to financing your home.

Most people don't have enough cash to pay for a house upfront, which is why they take out a mortgage loan. A mortgage is a type of loan used to buy or build a house, where the bank lends you money, and you agree to pay it back over time with interest. If you don't make your payments, the bank has the right to take back the house—so choosing the right mortgage is an important financial decision!

In this project, you will take on the role of an architect, engineer, and financial planner to design and build a new home while staying within a budget.

You will need to complete the following Project Phases:

- **Design Phase:** Use the sketch of a home layout that follows project criteria for rooms and extras.
- **Budgeting Phase:** Be assigned an initial budget of $100 with the option to increase the loan for your home.
- **Final Presentation:** Present your home design and explain your budgeting choices.

By the end of this project, you'll have a fully designed home model, just like real homeowners and builders do. But remember—just like in the real world, unexpected costs may arise, and you'll need to make smart financial choices!

Engineering Design Project: My New Construction Home

Goal: Ask the participants what is an acceptable goal for building a house. Make sure they realize that they need to think about what the house will be able to do once built and add that to the goal.

Build a new house with all the rooms and features you want while staying within your budget for building your new home.

Ask/Imagine Stage: Have the participants ask questions about the project. You should answer questions on what materials they can use, the criteria for the project, any constraints they may have with the project, and how they can test the project and know if it works or does not work.

Build a new house with all the rooms and features you want while staying within your budget out of materials provided:

- Recyclable Materials (Like bottle caps, aluminum foil, parchment paper, newspaper, etc.)
- Decorating supplies like stickers, gems, glitter, etc.
- Engineering Supplies like popsicle sticks, pipe cleaners, straws, string, etc.
- Art Supplies like washy tape, stamps, pom poms, different paper, etc.
- Anything else you think they would love to build with

Materials to help build but will not be used as part of your design.

- Tape, scissors, crayons, markers, glue, etc.

Explain when engineers work their supplies are limited, so they have to plan for a small amount of supplies.

Criteria:

- The house must include 3 bedrooms, 2 bathrooms, 1 kitchen + dining spot, and 1 living area.
- The house must have a stable structure that can stand on its own. This includes a strong foundation, sturdy roof, and a window in each room for fire safety.
- The design must fit within the given land space.
- OPTIONAL: The house must include at least one additional feature (e.g., a deck, garage, or backyard).

Constraints:

- Use only the materials as specified.
- The house must fit within the designated plot size.
- The design must be structurally sound and able to stand on its own.
- The number of rooms and features must stay within the budgeted cost.
- The total construction cost must not exceed $500.

Test:

- Check if the total construction cost stays within the assigned budget.
- Ensure the house structure stands on its own without collapsing.
- Assess whether the final construction meets the criteria.

Plan

Note to Coach: This is optional since some younger participants may have trouble planning at this time. You can ask each participant questions about what materials they will use to build their house and how much. You can also use the example blueprint to show how a house may be constructed on the inside.

For the Plan section, you will have the participants create a blueprint for their home. Have the participants draw out the floor plan for their home. You can ask engagement questions like: What features would you want in a dream home? What factors do you think affect the cost of a home?

They should have the following showing on the plan: 3 bedrooms, 2 bathrooms, 1 kitchen + dining spot, and 1 living area; a strong foundation, sturdy roof, and a window in each room for fire safety; OPTIONAL - at least one additional feature (e.g., a deck, garage, or backyard). The final plan must be presented with a floor plan as best as they can.

Help participants weigh their wants vs. needs in home construction. Guide them in understanding financial trade-offs (e.g., a bigger house means higher costs).

Once participants have completed their plan, they must seek approval from the teacher before beginning to build. You can use a sticker or a simple check mark to write on their plan as approval. Confirm that all required rooms and features (e.g., bedrooms, bathrooms, kitchen) are included in the design. Review the blueprint to make sure the house fits within the given plot size.

My Engineering Design Process

Did it work?
YES: How can it be better?
NO: How can we fix it?

What do we have to work with and what do we want it to do?

Improve

Ask

The Goal:

What have we learned to complete this challenge?

Create

Imagine

Build it!

Plan

Draw out a few ideas on how to complete this challenge:

My Engineering Design Plan

Material	Properties	How could you use it in your design?

Draw a possible solution:

My Home Blueprint

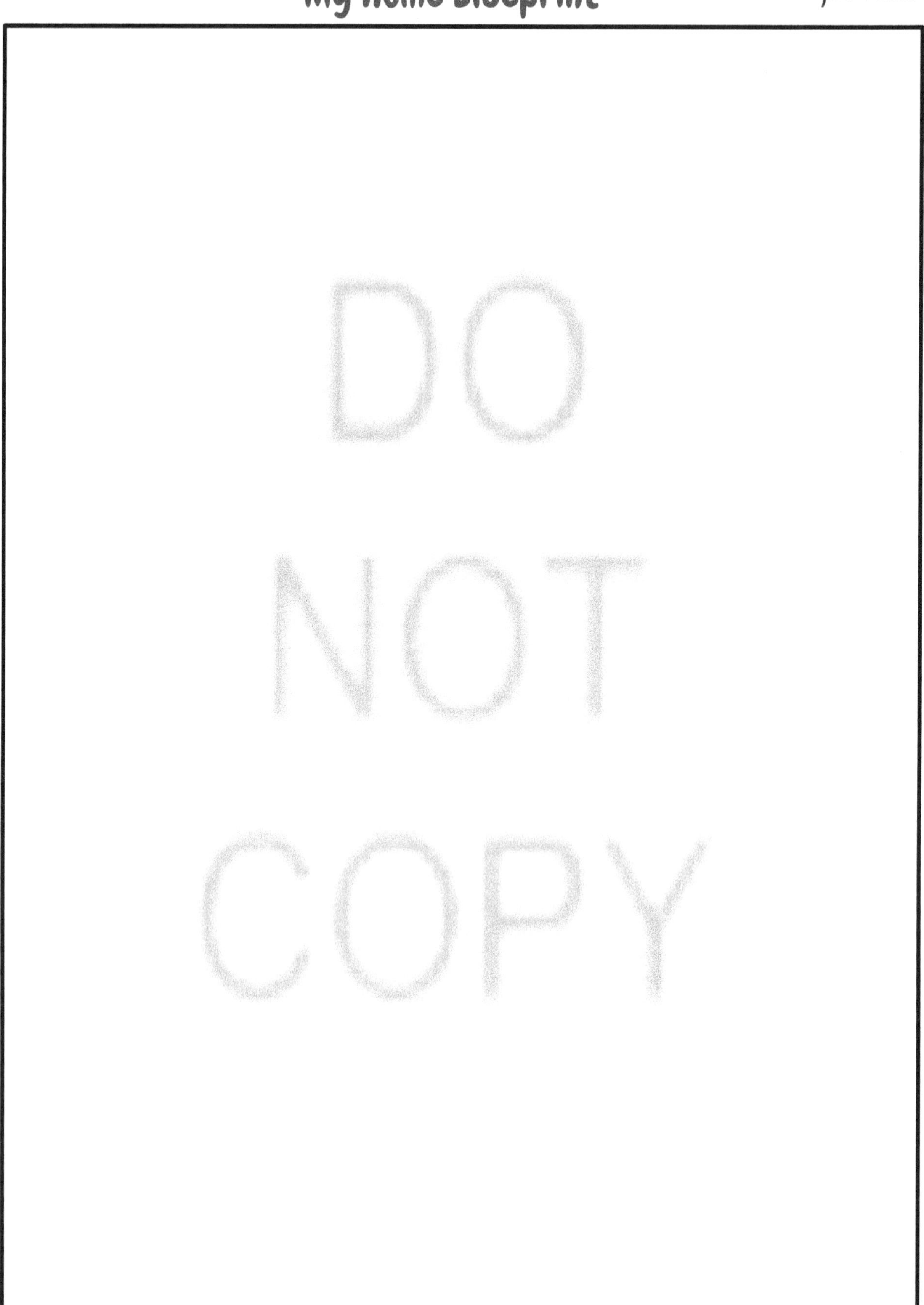

STEM for kids

My Home Blueprint Sample

Build

Set up the STEM Store - You can find the instructions in Module 3 Activity 3 of this course. Only follow the instructions for setting up the STEM Store and purchasing.

Allow participants to construct their home model. They should purchase the materials they want with the play money provided. They should bring their blueprints to life by constructing a 3D model of their home. They should consider the structure stability, room arrangement, and proportionality. Encourage them to be creative - They should add windows, doors, and furniture details.

Make sure participants ensure that they stay within their budget. If they exceed their budget, the participants will need to adjust their design or apply for a mortgage loan to cover the extra costs.

The mortgage loan requires an interview application to the STEM Bank - They will be asked questions about how they plan to spend their money and how much of a loan do they think they may need to complete building their new house.

Note to Coach: You may use the house template for younger participants to build their own house. They should make the furniture and people to go inside of the house.

My Home Template

STEM for kids

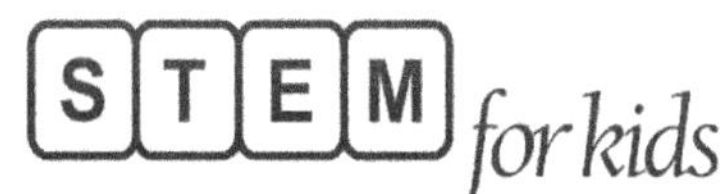

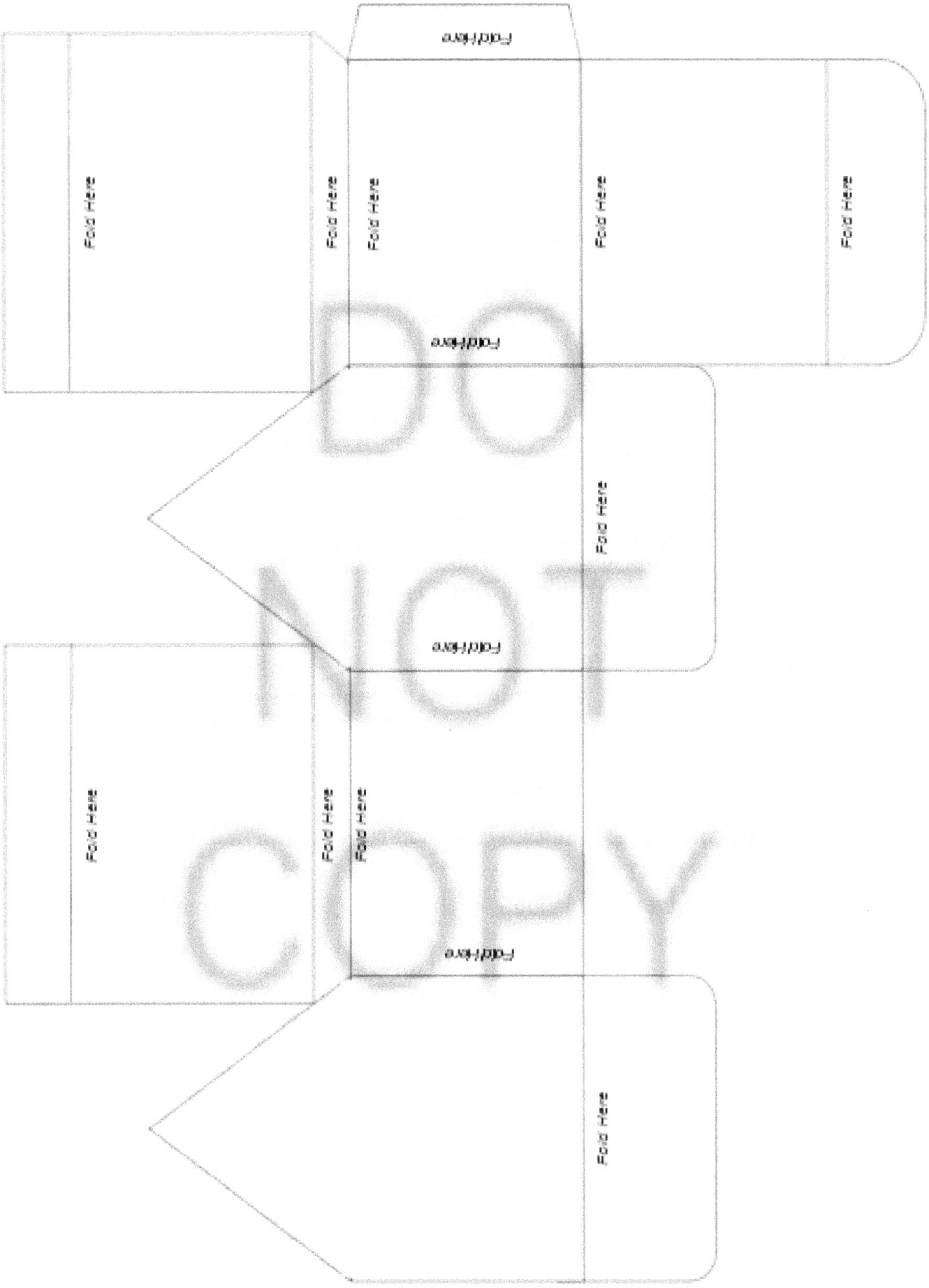
Fold Here
Fold Here
Fold Here
Fold Here
Fold Here
Fold Here
Fold Here
Fold Here
Fold Here
Fold Here
Fold Here
Fold Here
Fold Here
Fold Here

Test

Once construction is complete, have the participants test the integrity of their houses:

- **Weight Test** – Place a small weighted object (such as a small toy) on the roof to see if it can support additional load without collapsing.
- **Wind Test** – Use a fan or blow air at the house to simulate strong winds and check if it remains standing.
- **Shake Test** (Earthquake Simulation) – Gently shake the surface the house is built on to see if the structure remains intact.
- **Waterproofing Test** – Lightly spray or drip water onto the roof and walls to check if there are leaks (simulating rain conditions).
- **Foundation Strength Test** – Apply light pressure on different sides of the house to see if it tilts or collapses, ensuring a strong base.
- **Door and Window Stability Test** – If students include doors and windows in their design, check if they function properly without breaking or causing the structure to weaken.

Improve

After testing the structural integrity of their homes, participants should analyze what worked well and what could be improved. Encourage them to reflect on the test results and make modifications to strengthen their designs.

Ways to Improve:

- **Reinforce Weak Areas** – If the home failed the weight or shake test, consider adding extra supports or a stronger foundation.
- **Improve Wind Resistance** – Adjust the roof angle or add stabilizing features to withstand wind forces.
- **Enhance Waterproofing** – Use different materials or design features like sloped roofs to prevent leaks.
- **Optimize Space Usage** – Reevaluate room layouts to ensure an efficient and functional home design.

Encourage participants to apply these improvements and retest their homes to see if their modifications make a difference!

Reflection

Participants should now have a physical model of their home. Allow the participants to reflect on their project by testing their knowledge of budgeting. Encourage participants to document their reflections in a journal, group presentation, or classroom discussion!

Ways to reflect on the home build project:

- **Group Discussion** – Have participants share what went well, what challenges they faced, and how they overcame them.
- **Budget Review** – Reflect on whether they stayed within budget and how financial decisions impacted their home design.
- **Engineering Design Reflection** – Discuss how the engineering design process helped improve their home's structure and functionality.
- **Testing Results** – Review how well their home withstood the structural tests and what design elements contributed to its success or failure.
- **Improvement Brainstorm** – Think about what they would change if they could rebuild their home with a new approach or budget.
- **Career Connection** – Reflect on how engineers, architects, and financial planners use these concepts in real-world home construction.

4.9 Virtual - My New Construction Home

Time Required	**60+ min**
Group Sizes	**1**
Grade	**K - 8**
Materials Needed	
• Whiteboard/Markers • Laptop/Projector • Device for Each Participant • Play Money	

Learning Objective

- Financial Literacy & Budgeting – Participants will create and manage a budget for building their Minecraft house, making strategic financial decisions based on needs, wants, and available funds.
- Problem-Solving & Adaptability – Participants will respond to in-game emergencies by adjusting their budget, deciding on loans, and finding ways to manage unexpected expenses.
- Economic Principles & Resource Management – Participants will explore supply and demand, resource valuation, and the impact of loans and interest on financial planning through in-game transactions.

Explain to the participants that we are going to build a home in Minecraft. This home will be the place our Minecraft character goes to after working at their store or to place their materials they buy. You can have the participants make their own house or work with a partner.

Have the participants design the home with what materials they want to use to make it. Each participant will have $100 to spend to make their home. This includes the home itself and everything inside of the home.

Have the participants draw out a plan on how big the home will be and what materials they will use. Once approved, they can begin building the house with their budget provided on Minecraft.

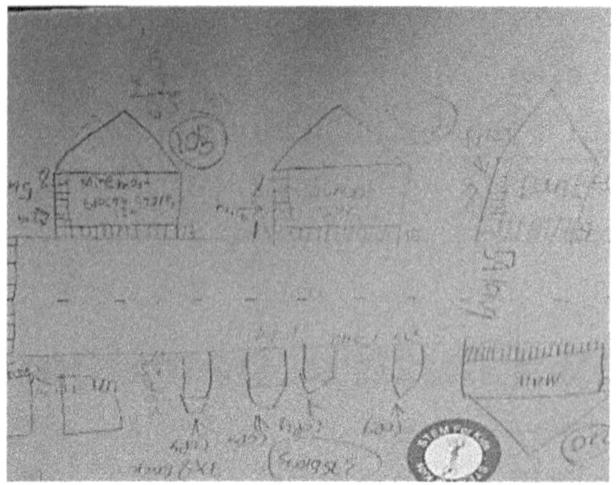

The only way the participants can get certain materials is by buying the materials from someone called "The Material Contractor." The coach will be the Material Contractor. The Material Contractor can give the participants the materials they want only if the participants send them an email stating what they want, how much they want of that material, and why they need it. Depending on the material, the Material Contractor will let the participant know how much their order is and whether they can get the material.

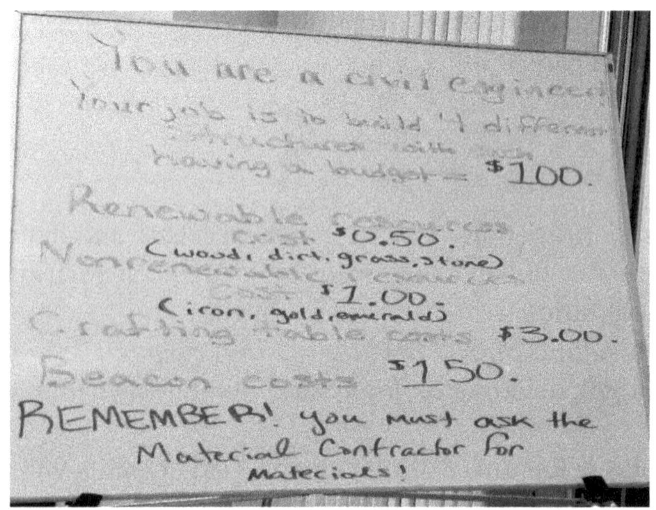

Make sure to have a pricing scale for materials. Renewable resources, or things we can always find more of, will be a low price such as 25 to 50 cents. Nonrenewable resources, or things we have a small supply of, will cost more such as $1 to $1.50. You have the freedom to pick the starting price however you like.

Also, have the option for the participants to buy premade tools (depending on tool, a wooden pickaxe would be $3 but a diamond pickaxe would be more) and crafting tables to save time and money.

For example, say a participant wanted to have 15 wooden blocks and a crafting table. First, the participant would have their budget at hand. Normally, the budget is $100. Renewable resources are priced at $0.50 and nonrenewable resources are priced at $1.00. Crafting tables are $4.00.

Note to Coach: It is a great idea to have artificial currency at hand so that it feels as if the participants are paying for their materials. Make sure to hand different bills out to equal $100.

Using the worksheet, the participant will state which material they would like to buy, how much of that material they would like to buy, why they would like to buy the material, and how much it comes up to.

Make sure the participants remember the difference between needs and wants. When they are building their house with a budget, they will want to create a plan on what to spend their money on. If they see that they are under budget, they may spend the remainder on a want or save it for a need later. If they see that they are over budget, they may want to re-evaluate what they are spending money on.

Keep Minecraft On Budget!

Use your knowledge to decide what is a need or want when building a house in Minecraft. Budget what you spend with your Minecraft money. Your budget is: $100

One Word Summary of Money	How Much Money Do I Have?	How I Got the Money
House Budget	$100	Savings from what I earned
All Money Together	**$100**	**All my money added up**
Things I Want to Buy to Build a House	**How Much Does It Cost?**	**Why I Want to Buy It (Need or Want)**
What It All Costs		**Everything I want to buy together**
Do I Have Enough Money?		**(Money – Cost)**

The example participant would like to buy 15 wooden blocks to make sure the base of the skyscraper they are building is stable and a crafting table to help with creating new tools and technologies with simple materials.

They calculated that the cost would be $11.50. With approval, you can then exchange the money and, using the Give command on the server menu, give the participant the materials they want.

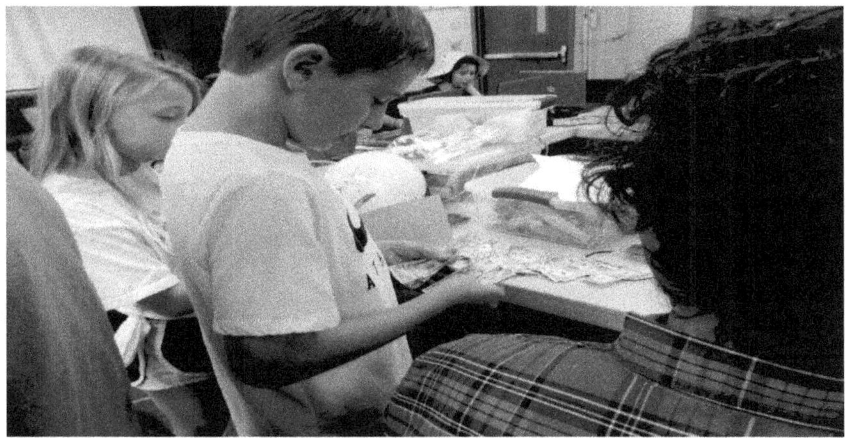

Note to Coach: Participants may ask how much a beacon would be. The price is set for $150 as it helps them move and build faster. Suggest pooling in money with the others in the group for the benefits. You can even have the participants write up a pitch for the whole group.

Note to Coach: Participants will ask you how to make certain items. The following page is a cheat sheet for you with all the recipes for items that we found were important for the projects.

As the participants are building their houses in Minecraft, they may run into a problem of not enough money. Let them know that the STEM Bank is currently accepting applications for personal loans. This means they can apply for a personal loan to receive more money to build their house.

There's a catch with loans. The STEM Bank has certain amounts of loans available with a participant interest rate. They will need to decide which loan fits their needs for finishing their house.

Use the worksheet below for the participants to decide which loan they want to take to finish their house.

STEM Bank Loans

Choose the loan that you wish to take out from the STEM Bank. Look closely at the amount of the loan as well as the interest rate. Choose only one loan.

STEM Loan #1

Amount Borrowed: $100

Term: 6 Hours *(Pay every 30 minutes)*

Rate: 30%

Payment per 30 minutes:

____

Interest / Fees: ________

Total Payments: ________

STEM Loan #2

Amount Borrowed: $200

Term: 12 Hours *(Pay every 30 minutes)*

Rate: 10%

Payment per 30 minutes:

____

Interest / Fees: ________

Total Payments: ________

STEM Loan #3

Amount Borrowed: $50

Term: 6 Hours *(Pay every 30 minutes)*

Rate: 15%

Payment per 30 minutes:

____

Interest / Fees: ________

Total Payments: ________

Loan Chosen:

____

<u>Signatures</u>

____

____

Once the house is ready, participants can go about their day by working at their job, relaxing, or going on an adventure. Give them time to add to their house and "live" in it.

After some time enjoying their house, let the participants know that an emergency has occurred in their house! Hand each participant a slip with a certain situation on it. Each situation will have the amount that it will cost to fix the emergency.

Here are some emergency situations that could happen:

- **Creeper Explosion** – A creeper destroys a significant portion of the player's house, requiring urgent rebuilding.
- **Fire Damage** – Lightning strikes, lava, or accidental fire burns down the home, leaving the player without shelter.
- **Villager Raid Aftermath** – A raid wipes out nearby resources, forcing the player to take out a loan to rebuild and restock.
- **Enderman Theft** – Key building blocks go missing due to Endermen stealing them, requiring urgent material replacement.
- **Flooding or Water Damage** – Accidental water spills (from ocean flooding or broken water sources) ruin redstone circuits and wooden structures.
- **Mining Disaster** – Falling into lava or an explosion causes the loss of all valuable building materials, requiring financial assistance to replace them.
- **Stronghold or Dungeon Damage** – Building near a stronghold or dungeon leads to excessive mob damage, forcing costly defensive upgrades.
- **Biome Relocation** – The player realizes their current location is unsuitable (e.g., too many hostile mobs, lack of resources) and needs a loan to move and rebuild.

Participants will need to create a new budget that has this emergency in it to see how much money they will have left for the day. Make sure they remember the loan they took out and the payments they need to make.

In order to have enough money for everything they need to spend in a day, they will need to either cut spending somewhere or increase their income. To cut spending, they need to decide what they do not need to buy for that day. For increasing their income, they need to either talk to the owner of the store for more time working or a pay raise.

Use the worksheet below to help them budget their new spending for the day.

Budgeting an Emergency!

Use your knowledge to decide if you will have enough money to fix an emergency.

One Word Summary of Money	How Much Money Do I Have?	How I Got the Money
All Money Together		**All my money added up**
Things that I will Spend Money On Today	**How Much Does It Cost?**	**Why I am Buying It (Need or Want)**
What It All Costs		**Everything I want to buy together**
Do I Have Enough Money?		**(Money – Cost)**

4.10 Mortgage Loan Analysis

Time Required	30 - 45 min
Group Sizes	1
Grade	3 - 8
Materials Needed	
• Whiteboard/Markers • Laptop/Projector • Device for each participant	

Learning Objective

- Understand Mortgage Basics – Participants will define a mortgage loan, explain the importance of a down payment, and calculate the loan amount required to purchase a home.
- Calculate Monthly Mortgage Payments – Participants will use Python and the NumPy .pmt() function to compute monthly mortgage payments based on interest rates and loan terms.
- Analyze Loan Payments – Participants will break down their first mortgage payment to determine how much goes toward interest versus principal and discuss how loan structures impact homeownership equity over time.

Let the participants know that they have been working as a data analyst for a few years. They are expecting a child soon, and it is time to start looking for a home!

They currently live in an apartment in New York City, but since they have been saving every month, they are able to purchase a home close by.

The home they are going to purchase is in the $800,000 range. While they do have a considerable amount of cash on hand, they do not have enough to purchase the entire home outright. This means they will need to take the remaining balance out as a mortgage loan.

Ask the participants if they have ever heard of a mortgage loan. If someone owns their home, it is more than likely that they have a mortgage to pay for their house. A mortgage is a promise to pay for a house but with the assumption that the bank can repossess the house if payments are not made.

They will need to put about 20% down up-front which is referred to as a down payment.

Participants will need to calculate how much the down payment is as well as the value of the mortgage loan after the down payment.

Note to Coach: You can use any software that allows you to code in Python. You may need to test your software first to be sure the code will work. The screenshots below use IntelliJ software. Another great web-based tool is https://trinket.io/ - You just need to have an account for students to use.

```
In [1]: import numpy as np
```

```
In [2]: home_value = 800000
        down_payment_percent = 0.20
```

```
In [3]: down_payment = (home_value * down_payment_percent)
        print("Initial Down Payment: " + str(down_payment))

        Initial Down Payment: 160000.0
```

```
In [4]: mortgage_loan = (home_value - down_payment)
        print("Mortgage Loan: " + str(mortgage_loan))

        Mortgage Loan: 640000.0
```

In[1]: This line imports the NumPy library.

In[2]: This line creates the variables for home value and the down payment percentage.

In[3]: This line prints out the down payment calculation from the formula.

In[4]: This line calculates the overall mortgage loan after the down payment is taken out. This is how much the loan will need to be from the bank.

Since the participants know the loan that they will get from the bank, they can now calculate the monthly mortgage payment they will have to make on a loan that size.

The participants will need to convert each of the parameters into their monthly equivalents. The interest rate will be tricky because it is compounding.

We are going to use a new function in NumPy called .pmt(rate, nper, pv) where:

- Rate = The monthly interest rate
- Nper = The number of payment periods (months) in the lifespan of the loan
- Pv = The total value of the loan

Let the participants know that they have been given a 30-year mortgage loan quote at 3.75%. They will use this information to figure out the monthly interest rate and the value of their monthly mortgage payment using the new NumPy function.

```
In [7]: mortgage_rate = 0.0375
        mortgage_rate_periodic = (1+mortgage_rate)**(1/12) - 1
```

```
In [8]: mortgage_payment_periods = 30*12
```

```
In [9]: periodic_mortgage_payment = -1*np.pmt(mortgage_rate_periodic, mortgage_payment_periods, mortgage_loan)
        print("Monthly Mortgage Payment: " + str(round(periodic_mortgage_payment, 2)))

        Monthly Mortgage Payment: 2941.13
```

In[4]: The first line sets the mortgage rate variable to 0.0375. The second line calculates the mortgage rate monthly.

In[5]: This line calculates the number of months within the period of the loan.

In[6]: This first line calculates the monthly mortgage payment amount using the np.pmt from NumPy. The second line prints the results.

As the participants begin the mortgage payments, they will start by paying mostly interest. This means that they retain very little principal which is the money going towards the ownership of their home.

If they were to stop paying their mortgage and sell their home after only a few years, the bank would own most of the home since they paid mostly interest and not the amount off the home.

Have the participants calculate the amount of the first loan payment that will go towards the mortgage interest based on the mortgage rate and calculate the remaining balance that goes towards the mortgage principal.

In [10]:
```
initial_interest_payment = mortgage_loan*mortgage_rate_periodic
print("Initial Interest Payment: " + str(round(initial_interest_payment, 2)))
```

Initial Interest Payment: 1966.43

In [12]:
```
initial_principal_payment = periodic_mortgage_payment - initial_interest_payment
print("Initial Principal Payment: " + str(round(initial_principal_payment, 2)))
```

Initial Principal Payment: 974.7

In[7]: These lines calculate the amount of the first loan payment that will go towards interest.

In[8]: These lines calculate the amount of the first loan payment that will go towards principal.

Once participants have calculated the amount that will go towards interest and principal, explain that this is something we must keep in mind when getting a loan. A loan can be a personal, mortgage, or school loan for this to apply.

4.11 Digital Repayment Plans

Time Required	20 - 30 min
Group Sizes	1
Grade	2 - 8
Materials Needed	
• Whiteboard/Markers • Laptop/Projector	

Learning Objective

- Evaluate Digital Repayment Plans – Compare different repayment options based on interest rates, terms, and total costs to make informed financial decisions.
- Apply Budgeting and Decision-Making Skills – Calculate affordability and select the best repayment plan based on their budget and financial priorities.
- Understand Financial Impacts – Analyze how digital repayment plans affect debt, credit scores, and overall financial health.

In today's digital economy, consumers have more flexibility than ever when making purchases, thanks to digital repayment plans. These plans allow buyers to split their payments into multiple installments rather than paying the full amount upfront.

Common options include "Pay in 4" services, which break a purchase into four equal payments over a set period, often without interest, and longer-term financing plans, which may include interest or additional fees.

While these options make large purchases more manageable, they also come with financial responsibilities, such as understanding repayment terms, potential interest rates, and the impact on personal budgets.

Learning how to evaluate and choose the best repayment plan is an essential skill for managing money wisely and avoiding unnecessary debt.

Place the participants into groups and have them discuss which repayment plan is best for their purchase. They will present their research to the class at the end.

Roleplay: Choosing the Best Digital Repayment Plan

1. Scenario Selection:

    a. Each participant (or group) is given a purchasing scenario, such as buying a laptop, gaming console, or household appliance.

        i. Gaming Console Purchase
            - You want to buy a new gaming console that costs $400.

        ii. Smartphone Upgrade
            - You need a new phone that costs $1,000.

        iii. Laptop for School
            - A laptop costs $800, and you need it for school.

        iv. Holiday Shopping Spree
            - You're buying $300 worth of gifts at one store.

        v. Emergency Car Repair
            - Your car needs a $1,200 repair. You don't have enough savings.

    b. The purchase must be made using a digital repayment option, such as Pay in 4, a credit card installment plan, or a short-term loan with interest.

2. Loan Option Research & Comparison:

    a. Participants receive multiple loan offers with different terms (e.g., no interest if paid within 4 months, a 10% interest installment plan over 6 months, or a longer-term financing option with higher fees).
    b. They must calculate the total repayment amount, monthly payments, and any hidden fees.

3. Decision-Making & Justification:
    a. Participants analyze which repayment option is the most financially responsible based on factors like interest rates, total repayment cost, and affordability.
    b. They justify their decision by creating a short presentation, written report, or discussion outlining why they chose a specific repayment plan.

4. Reflection & Real-World Application:
    a. Participants reflect on how these digital repayment plans impact financial health, credit scores, and budgeting.
    b. They discuss when it's smart to use these options and when paying upfront might be a better financial choice.

Bonus Challenge: Find a real-world example of a digital repayment plan (such as Klarna, Afterpay, or Affirm) and compare its terms to the options in this worksheet. What differences or similarities do you notice?

Digital Repayment Plans 

Step 1: Understanding the Purchase

- What item or service are you purchasing? ______________________
- What is the total cost of the purchase? ______________________

Step 2: Exploring Loan Options

Below are three different repayment plan options offered for your purchase. Compare them carefully.

Plan Type	# of Payments	Payment Amount Each Installment	Interest Rate	Total Cost After Payments	Additional Fees?
Pay in 4	4	________	0%	________	No
Pay Over 6 Months	6	________	5%	________	Missed Payment = $5.00
12 Month Loan	12	________	10%	________	Annual Fee of $10

Step 3: Evaluating the Best Option

- Which plan has the lowest total cost? ______________________
- Which plan has the highest monthly payment? ______________________
- Which plan fits best within your current budget? Why?

  ____

  ____

  ____

- If the plan includes interest, how much extra will you pay over time?

  ____

- What happens if you miss a payment?

  ____

  ____

  ____

Step 4: Making a Decision

- Which repayment plan would you choose? Explain your reasoning.

____
____
____

- What factors influenced your choice? *(Examples: affordability, total cost, interest, flexibility)*

____
____
____

Step 5: Reflection

- How can digital repayment plans be helpful?

____
____
____

- What risks do digital repayment plans pose if not managed properly?

____
____
____

- What strategies can you use to ensure you make smart financial decisions when using payment plans?

____
____
____

4.12 Bond Data Analysis Challenge

Time Required	30 min
Group Sizes	1 class
Grade	3 - 8
Materials Needed	
• Laptop/Projector • Whiteboard/Markers • Device for each	

Learning Objective

- Understand Bond Investments: Learn how bonds work, including concepts like coupon rates, maturity, and yield to maturity (YTM).
- Interpret bond data, create visual comparisons, and evaluate different bonds to determine their potential returns.
- Use Python programming to analyze bond performance and justify their investment choices based on data.

Explain to the participants that we are going to take a look at bonds that we want to ultimately decide which is the best to pick.

Bonds are a form of borrowing. People can buy a specific bond which makes them a lender. Whoever they bought the bond from, either a company or the government, now has a loan from that lender. The company or government must repay the loan over time to the lender. Just like a loan, there is interest and yield that the lender can expect as profit from lending the money.

For example, say you bought a bond at $100 with a 5% coupon rate (=$5), and it will take 5 years to maturity. The price you pay today is $100 which means you are at -$100 to start. At year 1 to 4, you gain $5 from the coupon rate. At year 5 or the final year, you receive your original $100 back plus the $5 coupon rate for that year. Ultimately, you received back $125 from the bond. Look at the picture below to understand. You may draw this on the board.

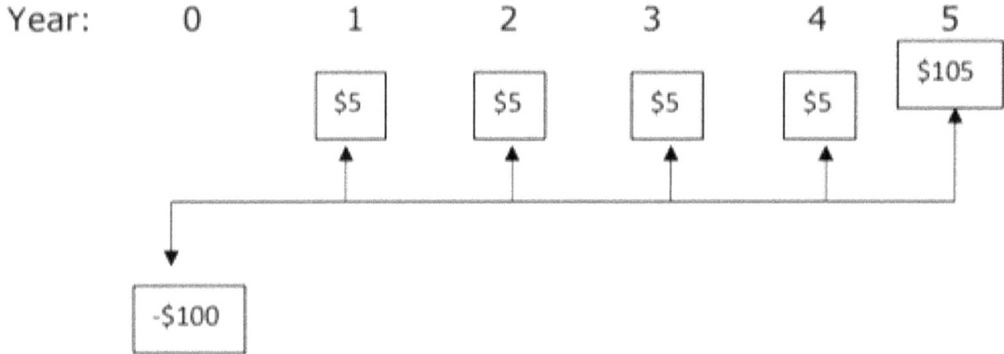

Let the participants know that they are about to buy a bond and want to find out which bond is the best to get. They need to analyze the bonds that are available to decide.

We will use the 4 example bonds to answer questions. These questions will start specific with us finding information and moving towards where there may not be a right or wrong answer.

Coupon Maturity	Kroll Ratings	Issue Description Call Information CUSIP	Price	APY/YTW	YTM	Qty/Min (M)	Action	Market Trade Date Settle Date
2.050 11-24-2020	B+	ALLY BK MIDVALE UTAH Non Callable CUSIP: 02006L6V0	98.685 98.841	2.766 2.681	2.766 2.681	2/1 10/5	Buy	Secondary
2.100 12-07-2020	B+	ALLY BK MIDVALE UTAH Non Callable CUSIP: 02006L7A5	99.340	2.452	2.452	6/6	Buy	Secondary
3.000 12-22-2020	B	GOLDMAN SACHS BK USA NY Callable, Next Call 06-22-2019 @ 100.000 CUSIP: 38148PR25	100.502	1.911	2.736	6/6	Buy	Secondary
2.300 12-23-2020	B+	AMERICAN EXPRESS CENTRN Non Callable CUSIP: 02587DL30	99.493	2.565	2.565	5/5	Buy	Secondary

The columns of importance are Coupon / Maturity, Issue Description, Price, and YTM (Year to Maturity).

The questions can be answered in many ways which means there is no correct answer for the participants to follow. Use what you know to get the answers. They can write the answer on a piece of paper or the whiteboard.

Specific Questions

- Based on the data, find the YTM of the bonds.
- Create a graph to compare the bonds and the gross amount.

Broad Questions

- Which bond is the best to pick based on the analysis above?

Once participants have written out the questions for them to answer, they may begin to answer using the Python programming tool. They should start with one question and show proof of their answer. Encourage the participants to come up with their own answers.

4.13 The Power of Giving

Time Required	30 min
Group Sizes	1
Grade	K - 8
Materials Needed	
• Whiteboard/Markers • Laptop/Projector • Bowls • Play Money	

Learning Objective

- Understand the Meaning of Giving – Participants will define what it means to give and explore different ways people share their time, money, or resources to help others.
- Evaluate the Impact of Donations – Participants will analyze how donations can positively affect individuals and communities by providing essential resources and support.
- Make Thoughtful Giving Decisions – Participants will practice budgeting their "charity money," considering trade-offs and priorities, and reflecting on how small acts of giving can lead to meaningful change.

Ask the participants:

> What does it mean to give? *"It means sharing what you have with someone who needs it." "Giving is helping people by giving them things they don't have." "It's when you do something nice for someone without expecting anything back." "It's like sharing your toys, but with bigger things like food or clothes."*
>
> Why do people donate money, items, or time? *"Because some people don't have enough, and it helps them." "So everyone can have what they need to be happy and safe." "Because it feels good to help others." "Because some people don't have homes or food, and we can help them get what they need."*

Show examples of different types of giving:

- Sharing Toys – Giving someone an old toy you don't play with anymore.
- Donating Clothes – Giving clothes that don't fit anymore to kids who need them.
- Helping a Friend – Carrying a friend's books or helping them with a task.
- Giving Food – Donating canned goods to a food drive or sharing a snack with a friend.
- Helping Around the House – Doing chores without being asked to help the family.
- Making Cards – Creating cards to cheer up someone who is sick or lonely.
- Donating Money – Putting coins in a charity jar or saving money to give to a good cause.
- Volunteering Time – Helping clean up a park, school, or playground.
- Helping Animals – Donating pet food to an animal shelter or helping take care of a pet.

Ask participants: How do donations impact people and communities? You can say: *Donations help people who don't have enough food, clothes, or toys. When people give, it makes others happy and helps them feel cared for. If a lot of people donate, it can help whole communities by making sure everyone has what they need, like food, school supplies, or a safe place to live. It also brings people together and makes the world a kinder place.*

Place multiple bowls around the classroom with a cause next to it. The cause paper should have a sentence about the cause's mission. Each participant receives a "charity budget" of $100 in play money. They will need to browse the donation opportunities and decide how to allocate their money, keeping in mind impact, personal values, and community needs.

Using the worksheet, participants will note down how they allocated their charity budget and explain why they chose to donate to certain causes, discussing trade-offs and priorities.

Once the worksheet is completed, have the participants answer the following questions: How did it feel to make charity decisions? How can small acts of giving create big changes? What is one real-life way to give back in your community this week?

Extension - Hands On Giving

Organize a real-life giving activity, such as…

- A **classroom donation drive** (collect canned goods, clothes, or school supplies).
- A **service project** (writing letters to hospitalized children, assembling care kits for shelters).
- A **mini fundraiser** (participants brainstorm creative ways to raise real money to donate).

Charity Opportunities

Animal Shelters

- **Needs:** Food, blankets, toys, cleaning supplies, medical care for rescued animals.
- **Donation Opportunities:**
  - $5 buys a toy or treats for a shelter pet.
  - $20 provides food for a rescued dog or cat for a week.
  - $50 covers vaccinations and medical checkups for one animal.

Food Banks

- **Needs:** Non-perishable food, fresh produce, meal kits, financial support for operations.
- **Donation Opportunities:**
  - $10 feeds a family for a day.
  - $25 provides a week's worth of groceries for a person in need.
  - $75 supports a holiday meal program for multiple families.

Schools in Need

- **Needs:** School supplies, books, technology, clothing, backpacks, meal programs.
- **Donation Opportunities:**
  - $10 buys a set of pencils, notebooks, and erasers for a student.
  - $50 buys school supplies for a child for an entire year.

Medical Research & Hospitals

- **Needs:** Funding for research, medical supplies, patient support programs.
- **Donation Opportunities:**
  - $25 helps fund cancer research to find new treatments.
  - $50 provides a care package for a child in the hospital.

Natural Disaster Relief

- **Needs:** Emergency shelter, food, clean water, hygiene supplies, rebuilding efforts.
- **Donation Opportunities:**
  - $10 provides a hygiene kit with soap, toothpaste, and other essentials.
  - $50 provides emergency shelter and blankets for a displaced family.

Homeless Shelters

- **Needs:** Warm clothing, hygiene kits, meals, temporary housing.
- **Donation Opportunities:**
  - $5 buys a warm pair of socks and gloves for someone in need.
  - $20 provides a hot meal and safe place to sleep for a homeless individual.
  - $50 helps support a shelter program for 4 days.

Environmental Conservation

- **Needs:** Tree planting, ocean cleanup, wildlife protection, sustainable farming.
- **Donation Opportunities:**
  - $10 plants a tree to help restore forests.
  - $25 supports ocean cleanup efforts to remove plastic waste.
  - $50 funds the protection of an endangered animal species for a month.

Veterans & Military Support

- **Needs:** Care packages, mental health services, job training, housing assistance.
- **Donation Opportunities:**
  - $15 provides a care package for a deployed soldier.
  - $50 helps provide counseling for a veteran.
  - $75 helps a veteran transition into stable housing and employment.

Children's Charities

- **Needs:** Toys, books, clothing, medical care, education support.
- **Donation Opportunities:**
  - $10 buys a new book for a child in foster care.
  - $30 provides a new toy for a child during the holidays.
  - $75 supports a child's medical expenses for a month.

Senior Assistance Programs

- **Needs:** Home care services, meal delivery, companionship programs.
- **Donation Opportunities:**
  - $15 delivers a warm meal to an elderly person in need.
  - $40 provides transportation for a senior to a medical appointment.
  - $75 helps fund home care assistance for a week.

Charity Budget Allocation

Step 1: Your Charity Budget

You have been given a budget of $100 to donate to different causes. Review the list of causes and their donation opportunities, then decide how you will allocate your funds.

Step 2: Allocate Your Budget

Fill in the table below with your donation choices. You can distribute your funds however you like, but make sure your total donation does not exceed $100.

Cause / Organization	Donation Amount	Reason for Choosing This Cause
Animal Shelters	______________	
Food Banks	______________	
Schools in Need	______________	
Medical Research	______________	
Disaster Relief	______________	
Homeless Shelters	______________	
Environmental Conservation	______________	
Veterans Support	______________	
Children's Charities	______________	
Senior Assistance Programs	______________	
TOTAL	______________	

Step 3: Reflection Questions

Answer the following questions about your donation decisions.

1. Why did you choose to donate to these specific causes?

2. Did you find it difficult to decide where to allocate your budget? Why or why not?

3. What were some trade-offs you had to consider while making your decisions?

4. If you had an unlimited budget, would you donate differently? How so?

5. How do you think donations like yours impact individuals and communities?

4.14 Future You & Retirement

Time Required	30 min
Group Sizes	1
Grade	K - 8
Materials Needed	
• Whiteboard/Markers • Laptop/Projector • Play Money • Envelopes • Index Cards • Dice • Art Supplies like Crayons, Markers, etc.	

Learning Objective

- Explain the importance of saving early for retirement and how different retirement plans, like pensions and 401(k)s, help build financial security.
- Compare the benefits and risks of pensions versus 401(k)s, including employer contributions, investment growth, and financial stability.
- Analyze how life events, economic factors, and spending habits impact retirement savings and determine if they can retire comfortably based on their financial choices.

Imagine if one day, your parents or grandparents didn't have to go to work anymore but still had enough money to buy food, pay for their home, and do fun things like travel or spend time with family. That's what retirement is!

Retirement is when a person stops working after many years of having a job. But how do they still have money if they're not working? That's where saving comes in! While people work, they set aside money in special accounts, like a 401(k) or a pension, so they have enough to live on when they retire. Some jobs even help by adding extra money to these savings.

Retirement is like planning for a long vacation—you need to save up so you can enjoy it without worrying about running out of money. The earlier someone starts saving, the more they'll have when it's time to retire!

Meet "Future You"

Each participant imagines themselves at 65 years old. They draw a picture of "Future You" and write down what they want their life to be like in retirement.

Future You

Imagine Your Future Self! Draw a picture of what you will look like in retirement (at 65+ years old) and what you hope to be doing during that time.

Where do you want to live when you retire? (City, Beach, Countryside, Mountains, etc.)

____

____

What kind of lifestyle do you want in retirement? (Travel, Hobbies, Volunteering, etc.)

____

____

What is one big goal you want to achieve during retirement?

____

____

Build Your Retirement Fund

This activity helps participants understand how pensions provide stable retirement income, while 401(k)s allow for more personal control but come with investment risks. It encourages strategic financial planning and highlights the importance of saving early for retirement.

1. **Getting a Job & Earning Income**
    a. At the start of the game, participants are 25 years old. Once they reach 65 years old, they can retire.

    b. Every round is a duration of 5 years. Meaning, after round 1, the participant is now 30 years old. It will take 8 rounds to retire.

    c. Each participant chooses a career with an assigned starting salary (e.g., teacher, engineer, artist). You can print off the career cards and have participants pick at random or you can have them pick their own career and do research on the starting salary for that career.
        i. They receive play money based on their salary every year. Divide by 1,000 to scale down the salary to a reasonable amount for the classroom simulation.
        ii. After they receive their assigned starting salary, have the participants calculate how much money in salary they receive every 5 years or in one round.
            - For example, if their annual salary is $100,000, first divide by 1,000 to scale down = $100 per year. After 5 years, they would receive $500 after each round.

2. **Choosing a Retirement Plan**
    a. Participants choose between a pension (where the employer contributes a set amount) or a 401(k) (where they choose how much to contribute, with an employer match).
        i. Hand out an envelope with either "Pension" or "401(k)" written on it at random. Each should have the set amount the employer will match.
            - Examples:
                a. For pension, their employer deposits 5% of their salary each year into the account that earns 5% interest.
                b. For 401(k), the participant contributes 5% of their salary to their 401(k) and their employer matches the full 5%, adding that contribution to the account.

b. Explain the following:
   i. Pension participants place a fixed portion of their salary into the "Pension Jar," and their employer contributes automatically.
   ii. 401(k) participants decide how much of their salary they want to contribute (e.g., 5%, 10%), and the employer matches a percentage. Their money is placed in their personal "401(k) Account."

3. **Investment Growth & Risks (For 401(k) Holders)**
   a. 401(k) participants roll a die at the end of each round to determine investment performance.
      i. Rolling a 1-2 means the market is down (no growth).
      ii. Rolling a 3-4 means moderate growth (add a small bonus to their savings like $1).
      iii. Rolling a 5-6 means strong growth (double their investment gains).

   b. Pension participants do not roll a die, as their retirement is guaranteed.

4. **Life Events**
   a. Draw "Life Event" cards that affect savings, such as a salary increase (allowing for higher contributions), an unexpected expense (forcing a participant to lower contributions), or an economic downturn (affecting 401(k) investments). Complete the task on that life event card.

5. **Reaching Retirement**
   a. After 8 rounds (simulating years of work), participants retire. Have them calculate how much money they saved for retirement.

   b. Pension holders receive a steady, guaranteed payout.

   c. 401(k) holders calculate their final balance and determine if they saved enough to retire comfortably.

6. **Can You Retire Comfortably?**
   a. Participants will receive a set of expenses in retirement:
      i. Housing ($1,500/month rent or mortgage)
      ii. Groceries ($400/month)
      iii. Healthcare ($600/month)
      iv. Leisure & Travel ($300/month)

   b. They will calculate their expected monthly retirement expenses.

c. Using a simple rule of thumb (e.g., "You need at least 25 times your annual expenses saved to retire comfortably"), participants will check if they have enough savings.
    i. Example: If their expected annual expenses are $40,000, they need at least $1 million in savings to retire comfortably.

d. Decision Time: Can They Retire?
    i. If they meet or exceed their retirement goal, they can retire comfortably!
    ii. If they fall short, they must decide:
        - Delay retirement and work a few more rounds to save more.
        - Cut expenses to live on less.
        - Take a part-time job in retirement.

Reflection questions you can ask the participants after this simulation:
- What were the benefits and risks of each retirement plan?
- How did employer contributions impact savings?
- How did life events affect retirement savings decisions?
- If you could go back, would you make different saving choices?

Extension: Play "The Game of Life" to recap the importance of financial literacy in real life.

Life Event Cards

Promotion You get a raise of $5,000 per year. Decide how much to put into your retirement.
Job Change You switch jobs and now have a different employer match policy (higher or lower). Grab a new job from the bowl.
Pay Cut Your salary decreases by $3,000 per year due to economic downturns. Adjust your savings plan.
Bonus You receive a $2,000 work bonus. Will you spend it or invest it for retirement?
Employer Match Increase Your company increases its retirement match from 3% to 6%.
Medical Emergency You have a big medical bill of $5,000. Where do you find the money? Hand the amount over to your teacher.
Car Breakdown Your car repair costs $2,500. Where do you find the money? Hand the amount over to your teacher.
Home Repair A major home repair costs you $4,000. Can you still contribute to retirement this year?
Stock Market Drop Your investments lose 10% of value. What do you do about retirement this year?

Stock Market Boom

Your investments gain 15%! Will you invest more or cash out some for a vacation?

Marriage

Your household income changes. Your partner makes $50,000 annually.
Any changes to be made to your retirement savings?

Baby on the Way

Expenses increase, but you also gain new tax benefits.
How does this impact retirement savings?

Child's College Fund

You decide to save for your child's education.
Does this affect your retirement savings?

Divorce

You must divide assets and adjust your financial plan.

Inheritance

You receive $10,000 from a family member. Will you save, invest, or spend it?

Early Retirement Offer

Your company offers you early retirement with a lump sum of $10,000.
Do you take it?

Delayed Retirement

You choose to work five extra years, increasing your retirement savings.

Downsizing Home in Retirement

You sell your home and move into a smaller one, freeing up cash for retirement.

Side Business in Retirement

You start a side hustle that brings in an extra $5,000 per year.
Will you invest in it?

4.15 Recap

Time Required	15 - 20 min
Group Sizes	1
Grade	K - 8
Materials Needed	
• Paper • Pencil • Whiteboard • Balloon • Permanent Marker	

Learning Objective

- Recall and apply terms and ideas related to finance, money, and engineering through an interactive activity.
- Provide an informal opportunity to evaluate participants' comprehension of key topics covered in class.
- Develop the ability to convey and recognize ideas through drawing and verbal explanation.
- Build teamwork and camaraderie by encouraging participants to work together during the game.

Using a balloon (or inflatable ball), write general questions on it (i.e. Name one fun thing you did today, Name one thing you learned today, Explain how you could use learning from today in your everyday life, etc.). Then toss the balloon/ball back and forth in a circle and whenever someone catches it, they have to answer the question that their left thumb is touching (or near).

You can play a game where each person bumps the ball to another person in a circle and, if a participant lets the ball hit the ground, they have to answer a review question. You can also play a musical chairs type of game where music will play as they toss the ball in a circle and whoever has the ball when the music pauses has to answer a question their hand is on.

Notes

Module 5: A Penny Saved

This module introduces key financial concepts such as saving, investing, and responsible money management. Participants will explore budgeting, delayed gratification, and the stock market while learning to allocate earnings, track spending, and set savings goals.

Materials

Materials for the Class:

- Laptop/Projector
- Scissors/Tape/Masking Tape/Glue
- Markers/Crayons/Pencils
- Art Supplies like stickers, washy tape, stamps, pom poms, etc.
- Prize of Your Choice
- Stapler

Materials for Each Child/Group:

- Pencil (1 per group / participant)
- Computer (1 per group / participant)
- Play Money
- Dice
- Recycled Materials
- Cardstock/Printer Paper

5.1 I've Got the Money!

Time Required	45 - 60 min
Group Sizes	1
Grade	K - 8
Materials Needed	
• Laptop/Projector • Whiteboard/Markers • Device for Each, Optional • Art Supplies, Optional	

Learning Objective

- Understand the importance of saving money and how a savings account helps manage future expenses.
- Learn how banks keep money safe, pay interest on savings, and use deposits to provide loans.
- Apply knowledge of saving by creating a story that demonstrates responsible money management and distinguishing between needs and wants.

Ask the participants if they know what a savings is. Explain that their parents will more than likely have savings. A savings is the result of putting money in a separate bank account to use at a later date. Instead of spending money immediately as you get it, you can be money smart and save it for later.

Have the participants brainstorm why they may want to save their money instead of spending it. Have them come up to the whiteboard and write their answers. Can buy little things later like a snack or movie trip, can save up for a big item for themselves or others, use for emergencies such as a jacket that was lost or a lock for their bike.

Explain that, once the participants have saved enough money, they may want to put their money into a savings account at a bank. Ask if anyone has heard of or been to a bank before. Banks keep your money safe. When you give your money to a bank, it is called a deposit.

When you have a savings account with a bank, the bank may pay you for every dollar you keep in the savings account! The money the bank pays you is called interest. It will pay you interest every month you keep the money in your savings account.

The reason banks pay you interest for having a savings account is because banks lend your money to other people. If someone does not have enough money saved up to buy something, they often borrow money from the bank to buy big things, like houses and cars. The bank lends them the money and expects the people to pay the money back and a little more money to the bank for the service.

This is a bank loan. Remind the participants what they learned in Module 3. Without money from people like you, banks would not have any money to lend.

Give the participants the following prompt:

> Create a movie animation, comic, or children's book that follows a main character on their journey to buy a product that uses money from their savings.
> Have them express what would be a need or a want when buying an item from the money saved.

Remind the participants on the whiteboard of the brainstorm they did earlier on how they should use the money saved. Have participants present their movies/comics/books when everyone is finished.

Savings Story Plan

Type of Project (Circle One): Movie Animation or Comic or Children's Book or Other:

____

What Objects / Characters / Media will I Use for My Story?

____
____
____

What will be the Story for My Project?

____
____
____
____
____
____

5.2 Buy Now or Save for Later?

Time Required	30 min
Group Sizes	1
Grade	K - 5
Materials Needed	
• Laptop/Projector • Whiteboard/Markers • Prize of Your Choice	

Learning Objective

- Participants will define delayed gratification and explain its benefits.
- Participants will make choices between immediate and delayed rewards and reflect on their decision-making process.
- Participants will identify personal goals and apply delayed gratification to achieve them.

Imagine you walk into a store and see your favorite toy or a delicious candy bar. You have just enough money to buy it right now—but wait! What if you could get something even bigger and better if you saved your money instead of spending it right away?

Ask the participants: Have you ever wanted to buy something right away but didn't have enough money? Have you ever saved money to buy something bigger or better later? What do you think is better—getting something small now or waiting for something bigger later?

Today, we're going to play a game that helps us learn about saving and waiting for better rewards instead of spending our money too quickly. This is called delayed gratification, which means choosing to wait for something better in the future instead of taking something small right away.

In this game, you'll have a choice:

- Take a small prize now (like one piece of candy)
- OR wait until the end of class and get a bigger prize (like three pieces of candy)!

Which will you choose? Will you grab the quick reward, or will you be patient and wait for something even better? Let's find out!

Present the Choice:

- Offer students an immediate small reward (e.g., 1 allergen-free candy or 5 minutes of play time with a classroom toy while others complete a worksheet) OR
- Give them the option to wait to receive a bigger reward (e.g. prize from the prize box or 10 minutes of play time with a classroom toy while others complete a worksheet).

Allow Students to Decide:

- Let each student make their choice individually. Have them complete part 1 of the worksheet. Have them place the worksheet on your table.
- Keep track of who chooses the immediate reward and who chooses to wait.
- Complete the choice during the designated time.

Observation Period:

- Hand out the worksheet for participants to complete during their designated time.
- As class continues, occasionally remind students who are waiting of the larger reward they will receive if they stay patient.

Have the participants discuss their worksheet with a peer that chose the opposite of them in the game. Have them present what their peer said on their worksheet to the class.

Key Takeaways:

- Waiting and saving can lead to bigger and better rewards.
- Spending money as soon as you get it may feel good at the moment, but saving allows you to afford something more valuable later.
- This is similar to real life—if you save your allowance or birthday money, you can buy something bigger and more meaningful instead of spending it all at once.

At the end of class after the game, ask the participants to share one thing they would like to save up money for instead of spending their money right away. Encourage them to think about a real-life situation where they can apply delayed gratification (e.g., saving for a new toy, a trip, or a special experience). Conclude by reminding them that being patient and making smart choices with money can help them achieve bigger goals in life.

Extension: Have students create a "Savings Goal Chart" where they write or draw something they want to save up for and track their progress.

Now or Later? Game

Part 1: Pick Your Choice

Your Choice: ____

Why did you choose this choice for the game?

____

____

____

Part 2: Reflection

Why did you decide to take your reward earlier instead of waiting for a better one later?

____

____

____

How did you feel when you chose the reward that was provided without waiting?

____

____

____

Was there any benefits to choosing the reward to be provided without waiting?

____

____

____

Looking back, do you feel satisfied with your decision to choose the reward now?

____

____

____

Do you think delayed gratification is important in achieving long-term goals?

____

____

____

Now or Later? Game

Part 1: Pick Your Choice

Your Choice: ____

Why did you choose this choice for the game?

____

____

____

Part 2: Reflection

Why did you decide to wait for the reward instead of taking it without waiting?

____

____

____

How did you feel when you waited for the reward?

____

____

____

Was there any benefits to choosing the reward to be provided later?

____

____

____

What did you learn about yourself through this experience of waiting?

____

____

____

Do you think delayed gratification is important in achieving long-term goals?

____

____

____

5.3 Introduction to Investing

Time Required	60 min
Group Sizes	1 class
Grade	2 - 8
Materials Needed	
• Laptop/Projector • Whiteboard/Markers • Play Money • Dice	

Learning Objective

- Understand the concept of investing: Learn how investing involves using money to buy stocks with the goal of growing it over time.
- Identify factors that influence stock prices: Explore the factors that cause stock prices to rise and fall, such as company performance and external events.
- Apply stock market concepts through simulation: Participate in a stock market simulation to practice buying, selling, and holding stocks while observing market changes.

Disclaimer: This material is for informational purposes only and should not be considered financial, investment, or legal advice. Investing involves risk, including the potential loss of principal. Past performance does not guarantee future results. Always conduct your own research or consult with a financial professional before making any investment decisions.

Begin by asking the participants: Have you ever heard of the stock market? What do you think it is? Why do you think people invest their money in stocks?

Investing is the process of putting your money into something that has the potential to grow in value over time. The goal of investing is to make your money work for you, rather than just keeping it in a savings account where it might not grow as quickly.

The Stock Market is a place where people buy and sell shares (or ownership) in companies. When you buy stocks, you're purchasing a small piece of a company. If that company does well, the value of your stock increases, and you can sell it later for a profit.

The information below is for you to summarize to the participants.

Risk of Investing

However, stock prices are not guaranteed to always go up. They can also go down, and you might lose money. Stock prices can fluctuate based on a variety of factors, and there is always a risk that the price could decrease, leading to a potential loss of money.

Factors that contribute to risk:

- Market Volatility:
  - The stock market can be unpredictable, with stock prices often rising and falling on a daily basis. Market volatility can be influenced by changes in the economy, interest rates, or even political events.
  - For example, a global crisis or recession can cause stock prices to drop rapidly across many industries.

- Company Performance:
  - The financial health and success of the company you're investing in directly affect its stock price. If a company faces difficulties—such as poor earnings reports, bad management, or loss of customers—its stock price may drop.
  - For instance, if a company like ToyCo announces lower-than-expected profits or product recalls, its stock might fall as investors lose confidence in its future.

- External Factors:
  - Factors outside of the company, such as economic downturns, changes in government policies (e.g., taxes, regulations), or changes in technology, can also impact stock prices. For example, if new environmental laws make it harder for a company to operate, its stock price might drop.
  - Additionally, global events like natural disasters or pandemics (e.g., COVID-19) can significantly affect stock prices.

- Investor Sentiment:
  - The feelings and actions of other investors can cause stock prices to rise or fall. Even rumors or emotional responses can move the market. If investors get scared or panicked, they might sell their shares, which could cause the stock price to fall.

Real-Life Example of Risk:
Blockbuster, once a giant in the movie rental industry, experienced a significant decline in stock value due to the rise of digital streaming services, especially Netflix. Despite being the dominant player in the market, Blockbuster failed to adapt to the changing technological landscape and consumer preferences.

In the early 2000s, Netflix began as a DVD rental service that later transitioned to streaming, which ultimately disrupted the movie rental industry. Blockbuster, on the other hand, continued with its physical rental stores and late fees, which caused its business to struggle.

Blockbuster's stock price plummeted as the company faced increased competition from Netflix and other streaming services. Investors who had bought Blockbuster stock when it was at its peak lost significant value as the company's market share and profitability dwindled.

Blockbuster's inability to innovate and adapt to new technology led to its downfall.

In investing, it's important to recognize that a company's ability to adapt to changes—like new technology, market trends, or consumer behavior—can have a major impact on the stock's value. If a company doesn't keep up, its stock price can drop dramatically.

Reward of Investing

While investing in stocks carries risks, the potential rewards can be significant if the company performs well and its stock price increases over time. The reward of investing comes from the possibility of earning a profit when you sell your stocks for more than you paid for them.

Factors that contribute to reward:

- Company Success:
  - When a company grows, becomes more profitable, or introduces innovative products, its stock price usually increases. As an investor, if you bought stock in that company early on, you could sell your shares for a higher price than you originally paid, making a profit.
  - For example, if you bought Nike stock before the company launched a successful new shoe line, the stock might have risen in value as more people bought the products and the company made more money.

- Market Growth:
  - When the economy is doing well, stock prices across the market tend to rise, leading to potential profits for investors. A booming economy, low interest rates, or strong consumer spending can all help increase stock values.
  - If the stock market overall is in a growth period, many companies may see their stock prices increase, which can benefit those who are invested in them.

- Dividends:
    - Some companies share part of their profits with their investors in the form of dividends. These are typically regular payments (quarterly or yearly) made to shareholders. While not all stocks pay dividends, those that do can offer an additional reward to investors.

- Long-Term Growth:
    - Long-term investing often leads to greater rewards. Some companies, such as Apple or Amazon, started as small businesses but grew over time into giants. Early investors in those companies saw their investments increase in value significantly over the years. This highlights the potential for substantial rewards from holding onto stocks over an extended period of time.

Real-Life Example of Reward:
Investors who bought Apple stock in the early 2000s saw incredible returns as the company revolutionized the tech industry with products like the iPhone and iPad. Apple's stock price increased drastically, and those who held onto their shares made large profits as the company grew in value.

<u>Summary of Risks and Rewards of Stock Market</u>

Risk
- The value of your investment can go up or down based on factors like market conditions, company performance, and external events. You could lose money if a company's stock price decreases.

Reward
- If a company does well, its stock price can go up, allowing you to sell your stock for a higher price than you paid, making a profit. Successful investments can lead to significant financial rewards, especially over time.

By understanding these risks and rewards, investors can make more informed decisions about where to put their money. While there is always some level of risk involved in the stock market, the potential for rewards can make investing a powerful way to grow wealth.

<u>More Real-Life Examples</u>

Feel free to discuss the stock market by bringing real-life examples of companies participants will recognize and might even buy from.

This is for you to summarize to the participants.

- Disney (DIS)
    - Why it's a good example: Disney is a popular company that many kids recognize through movies, theme parks, and TV shows. It's a great example to show how a company can grow and change over time.
    - Stock Trend: Over the years, Disney's stock price has gone up, especially when they bought Marvel, Lucasfilm (the makers of Star Wars), and Pixar. The stock also went up when they launched Disney+ streaming service, but there were times it dropped when they faced challenges like theme park closures during the pandemic.
    - Example to explain: Imagine Disney releasing a new blockbuster movie like "The Lion King" or opening a new ride at Disney World. When people love it, the company makes more money, and their stock price can go up. If something bad happens, like a movie not doing well or a park closing, the stock can go down.

- Nike (NKE)
    - Why it's a good example: Nike is well-known for its shoes and sportswear, which many kids wear for school or sports.
    - Stock Trend: Nike's stock has generally gone up over time, especially when they release popular products like new sneaker models or sign famous athletes to promote their brand. However, their stock price has dropped in the past during times when they faced competition or supply chain issues.
    - Example to explain: If Nike releases a new shoe that everyone loves, like a limited-edition sneaker, people rush to buy it. This excitement can make Nike's stock go up because the company sells more shoes and makes more money.

- Roblox (RBLX)
    - Why it's a good example: Roblox is an online game platform that many kids love, so it's easy to understand how their stock price can change.
    - Stock Trend: Roblox went public in 2021, and its stock price soared when people got excited about the future of online gaming. However, it has also gone down when fewer people played the game, or when the company faced challenges like not making enough money.
    - Example to explain: When Roblox adds new games that people love, more kids play, and Roblox makes more money. That excitement makes the stock price go up. But if fewer people play Roblox for a while, the stock price could drop.

These examples show how stock prices can go up or down depending on how well a company is doing and how people react to news, product releases, and other changes. You can use these to help the participants understand the basic concept that stock prices are not fixed—they change depending on many different factors.

Stock Market Simulation

Explain the Game Setup:

- Each participant will receive a set amount of play money (e.g., $500).
- They can "buy" stocks from a list of pretend companies with different stock prices. See slips.

How to Play:

- Buying Stocks:
    - Participants decide which stocks to buy using their play money.
    - For example, they might choose to buy 5 shares of **ToyCo** for $500.

- Roll the Dice:
    - At the start of each round (representing a "day" of the stock market), roll a dice that will change the stock prices. The dice could increase or decrease the stock values.
    - For example, if you roll a 4, **ToyCo** stock goes up by $20, or if you roll a 2, it goes down by $10.

- Selling or Holding Stocks:
    - After each round, students can decide whether to **sell** their stocks at the new price or **hold** onto them, hoping for a better price in future rounds.

- Tracking Stock Prices:
    - Use the whiteboard to track how the prices of each stock change each round.

Rounds:

- Play 5-6 rounds (or "days") to simulate the stock market activity.
- After each round, update the stock prices on the board and allow students to decide whether they want to buy, sell, or hold their stocks.

Final Results:

- At the end of the game, tally up the profits of each participant.

Discussion: Ask participants their opinions on the stock market based on the game.

- Why did stock prices go up or down?
    - Discuss the factors that influence stock prices, both in the simulation and in real life, such as market trends, company performance, and global events.

- What strategy worked best for you?
    - Ask participants whether they preferred to buy and sell quickly (short-term) or hold onto their stocks for longer periods (long-term). Discuss the different investment strategies, such as day trading versus long-term investing.

- Real-World Connection:
    - Talk about the importance of researching before investing and why it's important to understand the risks involved. Use examples of real-world stocks like Tesla or Nike and how different strategies might work in those markets.

Extension - Researching the Stock Market

Have students pick a real-life company (e.g., Apple, Nike, Tesla) and research its stock performance over the past year.

They should track the ups and downs of the stock price and write a short report about what influenced the price changes (e.g., new product launches, earnings reports, news events).

Have them present their findings to the class.

5.4 Trick 1 - Not One Bank... Four!

Time Required	60 min
Group Sizes	1 class
Grade	K - 5
Materials Needed	
• Laptop/Projector • Whiteboard/Markers • Recycled materials like boxes, bottles, etc. • Art Supplies like stickers, washy tape, stamps, pipe cleaners, pom poms, etc. • Scissors • Tape • Crayons / Markers	

Learning Objective

- Understand the concept of saving money: Learn how to organize their money into four categories—SAVE, SPEND, INVEST, and GIVE—to help manage finances for short-term and long-term goals.
- Apply engineering design principles: Use the Engineering Design Process (EDP) to create a piggy bank that meets specific criteria, including secure money storage and creative design.
- Develop creative problem-solving skills: Practice using limited materials to build a functional and creative piggy bank, encouraging resourcefulness and innovation.

Explain to the participants that the first trick to saving money is to have four little banks instead of one big bank.

Each bank will be labeled differently: SAVE, SPEND, INVEST, and GIVE.

A saving bank is created for money to be used later on larger items.

A spending bank is created for money to be used soon on everyday things.

An investing bank is created for money that will be used several years from now.

A giving bank is created for gifts to help others.

Hand each participant a small piggy bank for each. Have them label the bank to a specific type above. Participants can decorate the banks with stickers, photographs, and cut-outs from magazines. The pictures will show how the money will be used.

Note to Coach: You can either have the banks be made from recycled materials.

Participants can take these banks home to begin saving money based on the four banks instead of one!

Piggy Bank Engineering Design Challenge

Tell the participants that we will be using the EDP to design, build, and improve a piggy bank that they can use at home and in class.

Goal: Make a piggy bank using **at least 4** different materials provided.

Materials Provided:

- Recycled materials like boxes, bottles, etc.
- Art Supplies like stickers, washy tape, stamps, pipe cleaners, pom poms, etc.
- Scissors
- Tape
- Crayons / Markers

Explain when engineers work, their supplies are limited, so they have to plan their designs taking into account the small amount of supplies available. Common materials like markers, crayons, glue, scissors, etc are available.

Criteria:

- The piggy bank must be able to securely hold coins and/or paper money. It should have a slot for inserting money. The design should include a way to retrieve the money without breaking the bank.

- The piggy bank should have a unique or creative design (e.g., themed, colorful, animal-shaped, futuristic).

- The piggy bank should be sturdy enough to hold money without tipping over or breaking easily.

Constraints: Use only the materials provided. Use at least 4 different materials.

Test: Test by making sure you can place your classroom money in the piggy bank.

My Engineering Design Process

Did it work?
YES: How can it be better?
NO: How can we fix it?

What do we have to work with and what do we want it to do?

Improve

Ask

The Goal:

What have we learned to complete this challenge?

Create

Imagine

Build it!

Plan

Draw out a few ideas on how to complete this challenge:

My Engineering Design Plan

Material	Properties	How could you use it in your design?

Draw a possible solution:

5.5 Trick 2 - Set a Goal!

Time Required	20 - 30 min
Group Sizes	1 class
Grade	K - 5
Materials Needed	
• Laptop/Projector • Whiteboard/Markers • Device for each, optional	

Learning Objective

- Participants will understand that saving goals help them plan how much money to set aside each month to afford a desired item.
- Participants will practice calculating how much they need to save per week and per month to reach their savings goal within different timeframes.
- Participants will collaborate with a partner to research a product, determine its cost, and create a savings plan to achieve their goal.

Ask the participants if they know how much they should save each month. Not everyone is going to save the same amount! It all depends on what you are saving for.

Do any of the participants have a big item that they want to buy one day? Have the participants explain the item that they want and how much it is. We will use their examples to decide how much should be saved.

For example, say they want to buy a new bike. Their parents say that they need to save $100 before they will pay for the rest of the bike. It can be tough to earn $100 in a short amount of time. This is why we have saving goals!

Have the participants decide how much they should save each month if they want to buy the bike in four months. If they save $25 each month, they can buy it in 4 months. This is $6.25 a week. What about two months? They would need to save $50 a month. Ultimately, the more you save, the quicker you get the bike!

Have the participants research online a product that they want. This can be a toy or practical item. They can write the product and price on the board. Have them work with a partner to decide how much money they would need to save in a month, 2 months, 4 months, and a year in order to buy that product. They need to show how much to save each week and month.

Savings Plan

Product Research

What product do you want to buy? ______________________________________

How much does the product cost? _____________

The Plan

Decide how much money you would need to save each week and month to buy the product within different timeframes. Fill in the chart below.

Time Frame	Total Amount to Save	Amount to Save Each Week	Amount to Save Each Month
1 Month	____________	____________	____________
2 Months	____________	____________	____________
4 Months	____________	____________	____________
1 Year	____________	____________	____________

Reflection

How much would you need to save each week to buy this product in 1 month?

____

____

How would saving for 1 year compare to saving for 1 month in terms of the amount you would save each week?

____

____

What could you do to make saving easier (e.g., cutting back on small purchases, saving part of your allowance)?

____

____

5.6 Trick 3 - Save First!

Time Required	30 min
Group Sizes	1 class
Grade	K - 5
Materials Needed	
• Laptop/Projector • Whiteboard/Markers • Play Money • STEM Store	

Learning Objective

- Learn how to allocate their earnings by distributing money into different spending and saving categories before making purchases.
- Recognize the importance of saving first by setting aside money for future goals before spending on immediate wants.
- Practice making thoughtful purchasing choices while considering the impact on their long-term savings goals.

Have the participants imagine that they have their dream job. They have just been paid $50. Explain that they want to go to the STEM Store to buy some gifts for 3 of their friends.

Set up the STEM Store with the product slips. You can put multiple of the same item on the table. Have the products displayed nicely for customers to view with pricing on each product.

Allow participants to buy the products that they want. Once finished, explain that they will need to put money into their four banks that they created. They want to save for a ticket to an amusement park that is $100. Do they have enough money left over to save?

Our third trick has to do with saving first, not last. The first thing they should do is divide their money and put it into their four banks.

Spending money is easy. You can only spend money once.

For example, you spend your SPEND money to go to a movie. You have all your allowance in your pocket. You then spend $5.50 of your SAVE money on popcorn and soda. That money is now gone. You cannot get that money back to put away for a bigger item. You will now have to save for longer.

Once the participants understand that they need to save first, have them retry the previous scenario with $50.

Make sure they place their money first in their banks then go shopping at the STEM Store.

Remote Control Car
$30
Puzzle
$10
Friendship Bracelet
$5
Slime Making Kit
$15
Bluetooth Speaker
$25
Joke Book
$8
Water Bottle
$15
Plush Toy
$10

5.7 Trick 4 - Cut Expenses!

Time Required	20 - 30 min
Group Sizes	1 class
Grade	K - 5
Materials Needed	
• Laptop/Projector • Whiteboard/Markers • Cardstock • Printer Paper • Art Supplies • Stapler	

Learning Objective

- Learn to record their purchases in a money diary to better understand where their money goes.
- Reflect on their spending patterns to determine if their purchases align with their financial goals.
- Practice maintaining a money diary to make more informed and intentional financial decisions in the future.

Let the participants know that the fourth trick is to keep a Money Diary. A money diary is a book where you write down what you bought, when you bought it, how much it cost, and why you bought the item.

A money diary will teach you something about yourself. For example, you may find that you spend $5 a week on snacks from the vending machine. You can ask yourself if those snacks are worth the money or you would rather save the money for something else.

Let's create the book.

Note to Coach: You may create a book for each person or buy a premade book for them to write in.

1. Take one piece of colored cardstock and fold it in half "hamburger style." This will be the cover of our recap book.

2. Design a cover for the Money Diary. Remember to write who the book is by.

3. Take 8 white pages and fold them in half "hamburger style." These will be the pages inside of the book. Leave them blank for now.

4. Place the pages inside the book. At the middle of the book, staple the pages together right on the fold. This will allow you to open and close the book.

5. On the first page, have the participants draw out the following chart for 10 items they buy.

What is the Item?	When did you buy it?	How much did it cost?	Why did you buy it?

Have the participants use this money diary to write down what they bought in Trick 3 on activity 4 of this module. This will be used as an example for future purchases they make.

5.8 Motivational Speaker - Saving Money

Time Required	45 - 60 min
Group Sizes	1 class
Grade	K - 8
Materials Needed	
• Laptop/Projector • Whiteboard/Markers • Device for each	

Learning Objective

- Summarize and expand on the four money-saving tricks by creating two additional strategies for effective saving.
- Design and present a PowerPoint to motivate others to adopt smart saving habits through clear explanations and engaging visuals.
- Create a video ad demonstrating a money-saving trick to reinforce its importance and make their presentation more impactful.

In this activity, participants will design a PowerPoint to convince others of their tricks for saving money. Participants will imagine themselves as motivational speakers that must convince others to follow their tricks.

Have the participants write down the normal 4 tricks of saving money that they have learned. Prompt the participants to create two more tricks on saving money.

Once they have decided on two more tricks, they can begin building their PowerPoint. They will need to have slides for each trick as well as a video ad using one of the tricks to demonstrate to their audience how important that trick is.

Participants can use the Motivate Saving Money worksheet to record key ideas uncovered from their research during the program. Use the notes to create a PowerPoint Presentation and present to everyone else in the class at the end.

Motivate Saving Money Slide Deck

Slides	Description	Information on the Slide
1	Title Slide	Slide Deck Title: Presented by:
2 - 8	Content w/ Picture Slide (For Each Trick)	Tricks: 1. 2. 3. 4. 5. 6. Picture associated with each trick.
9	Video Ad for Trick	What trick will you show: Video associated with the trick.

5.9 Recap

Time Required	15 - 20 min
Group Sizes	1
Grade	K - 8
Materials Needed	
• Paper • Pencil • Whiteboard	

Learning Objective

- Recall and apply terms and ideas related to finance, money, and engineering.
- Provide an informal opportunity to evaluate participants' comprehension of key topics covered in class.

Complete the end of the program learning summary worksheet to reflect on the learning from the program regarding financial literacy.

STEM for kids

Learning Summary

Program Wrap-Up

In this program, I learned ______________________________

____

____

The most interesting activity was ______________________________

____

____

I liked it the most because ______________________________

____

____

Draw a picture of this activity:

Notes

Module 6: Money to Cryptocurrency

This module explores cryptocurrency, its differences from traditional money, and how blockchain securely records transactions. Participants will research various cryptocurrencies, their uses, and safety measures.

Materials

Materials for the Class:

- Laptop/Projector
- Scissors/Tape/Masking Tape/Glue
- Markers/Crayons/Pencils/Paper
- Art Supplies like stickers, washy tape, stamps, pom poms, etc.

Materials for Each Child/Group:

- Pencil (1 per group / participant)
- Computer (1 per group / participant)
- Building blocks (e.g., Lego bricks, wooden blocks, or any stackable items)
- Small slips of paper or sticky notes

6.1 Introduction to Cryptocurrency

<table>
<tr><td>Time Required</td><td>30 - 40 min</td></tr>
<tr><td>Group Sizes</td><td>1 - 3</td></tr>
<tr><td>Grade</td><td>K - 8</td></tr>
<tr><td colspan="2">Materials Needed</td></tr>
<tr><td colspan="2">• Laptop/Projector
• Whiteboard/Marker
• Building blocks (e.g., Lego bricks, wooden blocks, or any stackable items)
• Small slips of paper or sticky notes
• Markers or pens</td></tr>
</table>

Learning Objective

- Understand Digital Money: Students will be able to explain what cryptocurrency is and how it is different from regular money.
- Learn How Blockchain Works: Students will understand how transactions are recorded securely on a blockchain and why they cannot be changed.
- Recognize the Importance of Crypto Safety: Students will learn how to protect their cryptocurrency by keeping their private keys safe, avoiding scams, and using secure wallets.

Note to Coach: Cryptocurrency is a broad and evolving topic. This is meant to introduce the idea and to show how the world of finance is trending.

Have you ever played a video game where you earn coins or tokens to buy cool stuff? Imagine if those coins weren't just for the game but could be used in real life to buy things! That's kind of what cryptocurrency is like.

Cryptocurrency, or "crypto", is a special kind of digital money. Unlike the dollars or coins you use in your piggy bank, crypto only exists on computers and the internet. You can't hold it in your hand, but you can use it to buy things online or trade with others.

How Does It Work?

Imagine you and your friends love trading stickers. Instead of using regular money, you decide to create a special kind of magic money that only exists on the internet. That's kind of like cryptocurrency!

Step 1: Digital Coins Instead of Paper Money
Normal money, like dollars or coins, is made by governments and kept in banks. But crypto is digital—it lives on computers, not in your piggy bank.

Step 2: A Super Secure List (The Blockchain)
Now, imagine every time someone trades cryptocurrency for a sticker, you write it down in a big notebook that everyone can see but no one can change. This notebook is called a blockchain. It keeps track of every single trade so no one can cheat or erase history.

Example:

- You give your friend Alex 5 "CryptoCoins" for a cool sticker.
- That trade is written down in the notebook (blockchain).
- Later, Alex uses those 5 CryptoCoins to buy a toy from Jordan. That gets written down too.
- Everyone can see the notebook, so they know who owns what!

Step 3: Mining - The Math Puzzle Game
To keep things safe, computers around the world play a hard math puzzle game to add new transactions to the blockchain. The first computer to solve the puzzle gets a small reward—new crypto! This is called mining (but no pickaxes needed!).

Step 4: Crypto Wallets - Your Digital Piggy Bank
Just like you have a wallet for regular money, you need a crypto wallet to store your digital coins. It's like a super-safe secret box that only you can open with a special password (called a private key).

Step 5: Buying and Trading with Crypto

Once you have cryptocurrency, you can use it to:

- Buy things online (some stores accept crypto!)
- Trade with other people
- Save it for later, hoping its value goes up

Blockchain Building Blocks in Crypto

Introduction (5 minutes)

1. Begin by asking students: "Have you ever kept a diary or a list of something important?"
2. Connect their answers to the idea of a blockchain by explaining that it's like a special diary for tracking cryptocurrency transactions.
3. Use a simple analogy: "Imagine a magic notebook that everyone can see, but once you write something in it, no one can erase or change it. This keeps everything safe and honest!"

Explaining Blockchain Basics (5 minutes)

1. Explain that a blockchain is a chain of blocks, where each block holds information about a transaction (e.g., someone buying or selling with cryptocurrency).
2. Highlight that every new transaction adds a block to the chain, and once added, it stays there forever—no erasing or changing allowed!

Activity Setup (5 minutes)

1. Divide the class into small groups of 3-4 students.
2. Give each group a set of building blocks and slips of paper.
3. Explain that each block represents a "block" in the blockchain, and each slip of paper represents a "transaction."

Creating Transactions (10 minutes)

1. Ask each student to write a simple pretend transaction on a slip of paper.
2. Examples:
    a. "Billy traded 1 StarCoin for a sticker."
    b. "Mia bought a pencil with 2 StarCoins."
3. After writing, they fold the slip and place it inside or on top of a building block.

Building the Blockchain (10 minutes)

1. Begin with one block as the "first block" in the chain.
2. Have groups take turns stacking their blocks (with transactions inside) on top of each other, creating a chain.

3. As they add each block, encourage them to say: "I'm adding a new transaction to the blockchain!"
4. Reinforce that once a block is added, it can't be removed or altered, mimicking a real blockchain.

Discussion and Reflection (5 minutes)

1. After building the chain, ask students to try removing a block from the middle. Explain why this isn't allowed in a real blockchain—it's permanent to prevent cheating.
2. Discuss: "Why is it important to keep the record safe and unchangeable?" (Answer: It ensures honesty and trust.)

Why Do People Use Crypto?

There are many reasons as to why people opt to use cryptocurrency.

1. **No Banks Needed – You Are in Control!**
   Imagine you want to buy a toy online. Normally, you'd need a bank or a credit card to send money. But with cryptocurrency, you don't need a bank—you can send crypto directly to the person selling the toy!

   Example:
   - In a video game, you can send coins to your friend instantly, without asking a bank.
   - Cryptocurrency works the same way—you are in charge of your own money!

2. **Super Safe and Can't Be Cheated**
   Imagine playing a game where no one can cheat or change the score. That's how cryptocurrency works! Every transaction is recorded in a special digital notebook called the blockchain.

   Once something is written in the blockchain, no one can erase or change it. This means:
     - No one can steal your money by changing records.
     - No one can lie about sending or receiving money.
     - Everything is fair and honest!

3. **Fast and Works Anywhere in the World**
   Imagine you have a friend in another country. If you wanted to send them regular money, it might take days and cost extra fees. But with cryptocurrency, you can send it in just a few minutes!

Example:

- Think about how fast you can send an email or a text message.
- Crypto works like that for money—you can send it instantly, no matter where someone lives!

4. **Limited Supply – Like a Rare Collectible!**
   Some cryptocurrencies, like Bitcoin, have a limited amount—just like rare trading cards or special edition toys. Because there's only a certain number, people think they will become more valuable over time.

   Example:

   - If only 10 golden Pokémon cards exist in the world, they become super valuable!
   - Bitcoin is the same—there's a set number, so it might be worth more in the future.

5. **Fun and Future-Friendly**
   Many people believe cryptocurrency is the future of money. Some stores already accept Bitcoin for buying things, and new types of crypto are being created all the time.

   Some games even use cryptocurrency for buying special items. Imagine earning real money from playing your favorite game. That's already happening with some blockchain-based games.

Final Thought: Crypto is Like a Superpower!

With crypto, you get:

- ☑ Control over your own money
- ☑ A safe way to trade without cheating
- ☑ Fast, global payments
- ☑ A chance to be part of the future of money

But just like superheroes need to protect their secret identity, you have to be careful with crypto. Never share your secret wallet key, and always ask an adult for help.

Why Do We Need To Be Safe With Crypto?

While cryptocurrency is exciting, it's important to be safe and learn more before using it. Just like you wouldn't share your video game password, you have to keep your crypto information private!

Here's why crypto safety is super important and how you can protect yourself.

1. **Crypto is Like a Treasure Chest – Keep Your Key Safe!**
    a. Imagine you have a magical treasure chest full of golden coins. But instead of using a regular key, you have a special secret password (called a private key) that only you know.
    b. **Problem:** If someone gets your secret key, they can open your treasure chest and take all your coins!
    c. **Solution:** Never share your private key with anyone! It's like keeping your game password secret so no one can steal your account.

2. **No "Undo" Button – If You Lose It, It's Gone!**
    a. If you drop a dollar bill, you might be able to find it or ask someone for help. But with crypto, there's no customer service to call if you lose your money or send it to the wrong person.
    b. **Problem:** If you make a mistake, you can't get your money back—it's gone forever.
    c. **Solution:** Double-check everything before sending crypto and keep your secret key written down in a safe place (not just on your computer).

3. **Beware of Tricksters and Scammers!**
    a. Some people on the internet pretend to be friendly but are actually trying to steal crypto from others. They might say things like:
        - "Send me 1 Bitcoin, and I'll send you back 2!" (It's a trick—they won't send anything back!)
        - "Click this link to claim free crypto!" (The link could steal your secret key.)
        - "I'm from a crypto company, give me your password to help you." (No real company will ever ask for your password!)
    b. **Problem:** Scammers try to trick people into giving away their crypto.
    c. **Solution:** Never trust random messages online and always ask an adult if something seems suspicious.

4. **Some Crypto is Fake – Don't Get Fooled!**
    a. Just like fake toys or knock-off brands, there are fake cryptocurrencies that try to trick people. Some scammers create fake coins and convince people to buy them, but later, the coins disappear and are worth nothing!
    b. **Problem:** Some cryptocurrencies are scams, and you could lose your money.
    c. **Solution:** Only use well-known cryptocurrencies like Bitcoin and Ethereum and always research before buying.

5. **Hackers and Cyber Thieves – Protect Your Wallet!**
    a. Hackers are bad guys on computers who try to break into people's crypto wallets and steal their money. If you don't protect your wallet, it's like leaving your treasure chest wide open for them!
    b. **Problem:** Hackers can steal your crypto if your wallet isn't safe.
    c. **Solution:** Use a strong password and turn on extra security (like Two-Factor Authentication) to keep your wallet locked tight!

Crypto Safety Quiz

Pick the safest choice for each cryptocurrency scenario below by circling your answer. At the end, calculate how many questions you got correct. Each question is worth 1 point.

Level 1: The Secret Key Challenge

You just created a **crypto wallet**, and it gave you a **secret private key** (like a password). Now you have to decide:

- **Option A:** Write your private key on a sticky note and put it on your desk.
- **Option B:** Take a screenshot of your private key and save it on your phone.
- **Option C:** Write your private key on paper and store it in a safe place, like a locked drawer.

Level 2: The Free Crypto Trick

You get a message saying, **"Click here to get free Bitcoin!"** It looks exciting, but what should you do?

- **Option A:** Click the link and enter your private key to claim your prize.
- **Option B:** Ignore the message and tell an adult.
- **Option C:** Share the link with your friends so everyone can try it.

Level 3: The Hacker Trap

A hacker is trying to break into your crypto wallet! How do you **protect yourself**?

- **Option A:** Use a strong password and turn on Two-Factor Authentication (2FA).
- **Option B:** Use the password "123456" because it's easy to remember.
- **Option C:** Tell your password to a friend so they can help you log in.

Level 4: The Crypto Trade Decision

Your friend tells you about a **brand-new cryptocurrency** that no one has ever heard of and says, **"If you buy it now, you'll be rich!"** What do you do?

- **Option A:** Invest all your money right away because your friend said it's a good idea.
- **Option B:** Research the cryptocurrency first and ask an adult before making a decision.
- **Option C:** Send money to a random person online who promises to double it.

Level 5: Sending Crypto Safely

You're sending crypto to your friend for the first time. Before you send it, what should you do?

- **Option A:** Double-check their wallet address to make sure it's correct.
- **Option B:** Type the address quickly without checking because you're in a hurry.
- **Option C:** Send all your crypto in one big transaction, even though you've never done this before.

Final Score!

- **5/5 correct:** You're a **Crypto Safety Superhero**
- **3-4 correct:** You're a **Crypto Explorer**, but you need to be a little more careful!
- **0-2 correct:** Uh-oh! Let's go over the safety rules again before using crypto!

6.2 Popular Cryptocurrency Research

Time Required	45 - 60 min
Group Sizes	1 - 3
Grade	3 - 8
Materials Needed	
• Laptop/Projector • Whiteboard/Marker • Device for each • Poster Boards/Art Supplies, Optional	

Learning Objective

- Participants will identify and describe different types of cryptocurrency, including their purpose and unique features.
- Participants will research and present key facts about a specific cryptocurrency, demonstrating an understanding of its uses and potential risks.
- Participants will evaluate the role of cryptocurrency in the modern financial world and reflect on its benefits and challenges.

Note to coach: Cryptocurrency is a broad and evolving topic. This is meant to introduce the idea and to show how the world of finance is trending.

Let the participants know that, just like we have different types of regular money like dollars, euros, yen, etc., there are different types of cryptocurrency. Today, we are going to learn about a few popular cryptocurrencies and why people use them. You will research one cryptocurrency and present your findings to the group.

Assign Cryptocurrencies:
Divide students into small groups and assign (or let them choose) a popular cryptocurrency to research.

Some options:

- Bitcoin (BTC) – The first and most famous cryptocurrency.
- Ethereum (ETH) – Known for smart contracts and apps.
- Dogecoin (DOGE) – A meme/joke-based crypto.
- Solana (SOL) – Fast and popular for digital apps.
- Cardano (ADA) – Focuses on being eco-friendly.
- Polkadot (DOT) – Connects different blockchains.

Guiding Research Questions:
Students should find answers to and complete the worksheet:

- When was this cryptocurrency created, and by whom?
- What makes it special compared to other cryptocurrencies?
- How do people use it? (Buying things, trading, gaming, etc.)
- What is one fun fact about this cryptocurrency?
- What is one reason people should be careful when using it?

Research Methods:
Students can use kid-friendly research websites or any provided fact sheets you give out. Encourage them to take notes and highlight key information.

Create a Presentation:
Students will create a fun, simple presentation to share their research.

Options include:

- Poster Board: Draw the cryptocurrency's logo and key facts.
- Google Slides/PowerPoint: Create a short slide show with images and facts.

Presentation and Discussion:
Each group presents their findings in 2-3 minutes.

After each presentation, ask:

- "Would you want to use this cryptocurrency? Why or why not?"
- "What is something interesting you learned?"

Wrap-Up & Reflection:
Summarize key points:

- Different cryptocurrencies have different uses.
- Some are popular for trading, while others are used in apps or games.
- It's important to be careful and stay safe when using cryptocurrency.

End with a fun question: "If you could invent your own cryptocurrency, what would it be called and what would it do?"

Cryptocurrency Research Project

1. Basic Information

Cryptocurrency Name: ______________________________

When was this cryptocurrency created? ______________________________

Who created it? ____

Why was it created? ____

2. What Makes It Special?

What makes this cryptocurrency different from others?

____

____

Does it have any special features (faster, cheaper, used for apps/games, etc.)?

____

____

3. How Do People Use It?

What can you buy or do with this cryptocurrency?

☐ Buy things online
☐ Trade with others
☐ Play games
☐ Other: ____________________

Is this cryptocurrency more popular in certain countries or for specific uses?

____

4. Fun Fact!

Write one interesting or funny fact about this cryptocurrency:

____

5. Staying Safe with Crypto

What is one risk or danger when using this cryptocurrency?

____

____

How can people protect themselves from scams or mistakes?

____

____

www.ingramcontent.com/pod-product-compliance
Lightning Source LLC
Chambersburg PA
CBHW080414270326
41929CB00018B/3028

* 9 7 9 8 9 8 7 8 3 6 0 8 8 *